To Stacey

Everything begins first
with a dream! The wind
Allow "Spirit" to place the
under your wings to fly

Keep dreaming and
Smile!

Blessings,
Barbara
October 2007

CW01572525

The River of Dreams

Tools for Transforming Ordinary
Experiences Into Extraordinary Realities

Barbara Smith

authorHOUSE®

AuthorHouse™
1663 Liberty Drive, Suite 200
Bloomington, IN 47403
www.authorhouse.com
Phone: 1-800-839-8640

First published by AuthorHouse 9/4/2007

ISBN: 978-1-4343-2291-3 (sc)
ISBN: 978-1-4343-2292-0 (hc)

Library of Congress Control Number: 2007905166

Printed in the United States of America
Bloomington, Indiana

This book is printed on acid-free paper.

This book is dedicated

To my grandchildren:

Allison, Kylie and Quinn.

I share with you these words spoken to me by a man of great wisdom and spiritual leadership, Brother Ishmael Tetteh:

"If you do not have some fear,
then it is not a
dream."

If it does not seem impossible,
then it is not a
Dream."

I wish to say to you, my dear children,
"Have courage to face your fears and
dream the impossible!"

Table of Contents

Foreword ix

Acknowledgements xi

Introduction... 1

Part I: My Foundation

Chapter One: The Journey Begins 9

Chapter Two: Opening The Box 17

Chapter Three: Two Worlds 29

Chapter Four: Messages Come in Many Forms............. 37

Chapter Five: The Heartbeat Of The Mountain
Called To Me 47

Part II: Dream Messangers- Waking and Asleep

Chapter Six: Unpacking The Emotions 61

Chapter Seven: Tracking the Dreams 87

Chapter Eight: The Healer Within......................... 99

Chapter Nine: It's All In Our Perception.................... 113

Chapter Ten: Guidelines for Navigating the
River of Dreams 121

Chapter Eleven: Living In "Dreamland" 127

Foreword

$\mathcal{G}$ am delighted that Barbara Smith has written *The River of Dreams,* as it answers many questions people are likely to ask about dream recall. Barbara's book gave me a solid key to unlock powerful messages of living the awakened dream. Everyone dreams every night, and some people have difficulty recalling their dreams. Through Barbara's extensive experience of dream recall, she teaches and installs the message of paying attention and having a dreams journal beside our bed. She teaches that by journaling our dreams it facilitates healing and assists in helping our lives unfold for our highest good. Her message in this enchanting book is loud and clear, she tells us to pay attention to the messages we receive either in the dream-state or in our awakened times. We need to dream to be healthy and happy and to understand ourselves it is important to interpret our dreams.

Barbara's book enhances the question: "Have you ever wondered where all your brilliant ideas come from?"

Your spirit guides deliver a great deal of information to you while you are in the alpha (relaxed or dreaming) or the theta (deep sleep) state, at night or during meditation. They use such times to transmit advice, ideas, and suggestions to your subconscious mind.

Barbara Smith's own spiritual journey speaks to the reader of her dedication, hard work and profound inner-wisdom, and her words come with deep meaningful tips. Her book passes on messages of humility and a great depth of understanding for a peaceful self and a peaceful world.

Barbara's book reinstates the importance and powerful messages that are given to us in our dream state. This is the perfect book to help people to unravel, awaken and understand their dreams.

Reverend Jenny Crawford
Author of *Spirit of Love* and *Through the Eyes of Spirit*
Tauranga, (The Bay of Plenty) New Zealand

Acknowledments

This book is an acknowledgement to everyone who has touched my life. Your inspiration, teachings and support have been a part of creating these pages.

There are personal acknowledgments I also wish to offer to those that have traveled on the journey with me, in order to bring this book into manifestation. To my editor Eve Hogan, your devotion to this work was a divine gift. When the blocks showed up, and the mind got weary, you gently held the space for me to return in clarity. Your wisdom, guidance, and understanding of the creative process called writing, provided the insight and guidance that continued to inspire me. You believed in the dream, and supported the work and myself with your inner strength and your development-organizing skills. "You are a writer's dream." To my dearest friend and mentor Benny, I offer deepest thanks for repairing the broken pieces, many times over. Your blessings have given strength, wisdom and understanding in the unfolding of Spirit within. The words within these pages tell that story. Thank you Sunny Faessell-Oliver for always being there with clarity when the field became foggy. You saw the vision of this book long before I had the dream. Thanks for pushing the envelope with a gentle nudge. To my friend Ginny, who lives on the east coast and traveled the two worlds with me: thanks for answering the late night calls, and all the joys, tears and laughter; you were forever there. For my California Dreamers keep dreaming, laughing and loving. To Ron Berger, one who understands the moon, the stars, and the planets; timing is everything, a big cosmic thank you. Cindy, David, and Tony, your support and technical guidance is lovingly appreciated. Thank you Brad Tiery, at Author House Publishing, for checking in with me over the two years of writing this book. Your personal touch was a gift in bringing this forward. I wish to thank everyone at Author House who worked on the manuscript and helped bring this vision forward in order to inspire the dream in everyone. To Rose, who opens her home each week for our meditation group to meet, and to each one in our meditation family, thank you for all the prayers in support. A big hug and warm thank you to Joe and Nance Belton for pulling the pieces together with support and copy editing. Your time and generosity is an expression of love, a beautiful touch to bring this work to completion and new beginning. I offer sincere love and gratitude to my family and friends, who have always been and continue to be my teachers.

Introduction

Introduction

*"We must sleep with open eyes, we must dream with
our hands,
we must dream the dreams of a river seeking its course,
of the sun Dreaming its worlds."*

—*El Cantaro Roto/Octavio Paz*

I have been asked many times over how I came to live the adventuresome life I live and how I can manifest opportunities and open doors that at first seem to not even exist at all. People want to know how I can be joyful, happy, loving and at peace when I have a daughter facing a life-threatening illness and have endured a divorce after thirty-five years of marriage (or was that enduring thirty-five years of marriage which led to a divorce?) ... They want to know how I, an ordinary person, live such an extraordinary life. I've pondered the answer to these questions over and over and have finally come to the place of understanding that allows me to share this book.

I will guide you through my process: how I have transformed my own struggles into strengths, understanding, and wisdom. I share it so that others may realize that they can do the same. My journey has had many initiations and transitions from single to married to mother to divorced to single again. My journey will lead you through several conversions from Christianity, to Judaism, to Eastern Philosophies, which all have led me to the Unity of One. This has been my *journey to wholeness.*

A river of dreams continually winds throughout my story. If you look closely and listen in silence, with trust, you will hear the voice of wisdom with which the river speaks. Now it may be a far stretch for some of those that read these pages to comprehend a river with a voice. However, if you are willing to listen and to see from the *heart,* then you will hear the river and see the dreams that flow within that source. The exploration into dreams has been a guide to self-discovery. I have learned how to navigate through the turbulent waters of life.

This is not an easy journey on Earth, and on many levels it is a university in which we receive no PhD. But, we all do have to graduate at some point in time. While we are here, why not learn the lessons? Come journey with me as I reveal tools for rewriting your drama and creating a new stage on which to play! These are the tools that I used to open doors to new awareness and greater understanding. I have come to a place where I consciously seek my dreams rather than wait for spontaneous dreams to occur. You may call this *conscious dreaming.*

Since I am a deep believer in the power of story — in looking at our own personal mythology — I'm going to share my stories, my life experiences, my dreams and the messages of wisdom they revealed to me. Making sense of my life journey has led me into meditation, dream work, journaling, risk-taking and adventure; this is where I plan on leading you, as well. The process that I have used has been to ask for guidance, listen closely for clarity, and to always trust that Spirit would answer…in *divine timing*. I have also needed *a lot of patience*! You will find the use of these tools revealed repeatedly throughout this book.

The lands that I have traveled and the indigenous people that I have walked with in those lands were some of my teachers, mentors and guides that helped me to understand the wisdom that is held within nature. They have taught me to listen for the messages that come from the animals, and all the creatures that roam our earth. They are referred to as *"animal spirit guides"* by those who listen closely to the messages from the instinctual nature. They taught me to listen for wisdom that is revealed in my dreams. I continue to learn how to walk in balance.

Together, we will explore many levels of dreaming, both those that come during our nighttime voyage, and those that I refer to as the "waking dream." I look at many experiences in my life as a "waking dream." Through metaphor, I am able to see what is right in front of me at that moment and what is being asked or shown to me as another way of expression. Throughout my journey, as I continue to deepen my meditation practice, my dreams have become more vivid, with greater clarity and greater understanding. Through this process, I realized that I had to be honest with myself if I really wanted to move in the river and start to ride the rapids, as they say. I needed to take a look at the parts of myself that were hidden from view. Those parts we never like to look at, or even realize exist, I refer to as *"the shadow self."* Isn't it interesting how we can always find those parts in someone else!

A very wise teacher once asked me what I came to learn. My reply was that I wanted to learn how to live my outer, daily life, in the way my soul spoke to me from within. I did not want to feel limited in my expression of who I was or judged for my beliefs. My journey has been the unfolding of that expression, to bring my life with Spirit into balance with living a full life of expression in the physical world. I've taken everything I have learned up until now and made it my own, weaving the tapestry of my life. My wish for you is to find your own way to journey and use the tools that work for your transformation into wholeness. The process you develop will be uniquely yours. It will guide you to a place that is filled with gifts that you never realized were in the river that flows within you.

You will need a journal if you wish to raft the river of dreams as I have. Throughout this book you will find questions to guide you, exercises to try, and new territory to explore. Your journal will be a powerful tool and a constant companion on your journey.

> *"In creation it appears that*
> *God sleeps in the minerals,*
> *dreams in the flowers,*
> *awakens in the animals, and*
> *in man 'knows' that he is*
> *awake!"*
>
> *Paramahansa Yogananda*

Part 1:
My Foundation

TRANSCENDENCE

I realize the confinement of one's limitations,
And feel the hidden fear of exposing the true self.

Is the true self not worthy of being seen?

Must we work in the confines of the structured mind,
Within the views of outside worlds?

My inner voice teaches my heart to hear
And see what my eyes and ears cannot comprehend.

My heart transcends all perceptions.
I am set free to be the expansion of the Cosmos.

I listen and know I AM the expansion of
God.

Poem: from my personal journal, 1999
Barbara Ann Smith

Chapter One: The Journey Begins

"Nothing happens unless first a dream."

—Carl Sandburg

When a child sees what we have long forgotten, a hush becomes the forbidden and the child no longer remembers. Years pass and she now questions: *Who am I?* She no longer recalls that she once lived in the field of *all that exists*. Generation after generation the hush and the forbidden continue. Imagination falls short and it takes great effort to diminish what was so strong and natural. Years later, in the long journey of searching for the missing pieces of herself, she finds the inner voice returns. She called them whispers in the night. They were the voices that spoke to her in dreamtime.

When a child *can see,* what we have long forgotten as an adult, we can invite the creativity and imagination to be explored. We often are unable to remember how to see through the eyes of a child. The threads that I weave together, in order to share my story, come from the mended pieces of a child's vision and my perception as an adult today.

I was one of those children that had a wild and curious imagination and was given that label in a half-accepting way and half-forbidden way. I remember at a very early age being very creative with how I saw things. Being raised in the country and on farmland, I was given great resources to experiment with my creative imagination and to be adventurous. I had a daring side of me, perhaps a daring accompanied with that little devil known as curiosity. I once decided to test the truth of bulls being attracted to red. I went to find my special red jacket and away I traveled under the barbed-wire fencing. I was heading off to challenge my charming playmates—the bulls! They were unaware of my presence. I started to take my jacket off, just like I saw in the movies when bullfighters stepped into the arena. Now I had their attention! I suddenly realized I had gone too far, as not one but several bulls began to move toward me. I was not about to find out what happens to the bullfighter when he has more than one bull in the ring. Fear started to race through me as I headed back fiercely trying to locate the place in the fence I had entered. I was not about to turn around to see if my friends were still following behind. I made a mad dash straight ahead and under the wire fence. Yep, I just got in under the wire. Well, not quite, as I tore the jacket in several places, but I received no visible scars that would prove my adventure that day.

I also loved sitting in nature as the wonder of it all took me to a deep place of contemplation. At the age of seven or eight, I sat and wondered where I existed before I came to earth. I even thought about where I could have been before my parents *were born,* perhaps on some far off star. That kept me very busy in the days I spent alone on the farm and in the fields. Well, I never got the answer then, but I continued the search.

My mother was the protector and nurturer while my dad was the adventurer, the scientist and inventor. While my mother was tending to the home and caring for the beauty of the gardens that she created with flowers of many colors, my dad kept the fire glowing down in the basement. I remember it well. You see my dad was also a Scientific Glassblower and had a shop in the basement, which gave him the opportunity to be creative at home as well as at his work at General Electric lab and Corning in New York. He created some of the instruments that went into creating the first solar heating systems in the United States. He also created some of the instruments that went into our first Space Shuttle. Perhaps this is where I received my passion and curious nature, especially my curiosity about the stars! I would spend hours looking up at the sky wondering which star I came from. I would pick out the brightest one and dream of the star Sirius being my home. I'm a dreamer from way back, I guess.

Since I didn't know anything about my paternal grandfather, who died before I was born, I had to put the pieces together through the few stories my father told me and one newspaper article we had. I was never even shown a picture of him, and when asked about his nationality, no one would say. In fact, it seemed as if the topic was not welcomed. The stories I remember about my grandfather were always of great adventures, so it seems adventure runs in the family. My dad would say to me many times that *Annie Oakley was almost my grandmother.* You see, my grandfather had several professions. One profession was working in the *Wild Bill West Show.* My grandfather rode horses and most likely had other jobs within the circuit of the show. So, there was always the possibility that the story my dad told was true about my grandfather *dating Miss Annie Oakley! Wow*, I loved that story and thought of all the adventure that I could have been a part of. Can you imagine Annie Oakley as a Grandmother? I sure can! Talk about a strong powerful women—she was a sharpshooter back in the 1800's and was called "the very spirit of independence." Can you imagine having *that* blood running through your veins? Oh well, I guess my dad's storyteller-blood runs through these veins of mine.

My grandfather had also been a steeplejack worker and that was the one that landed in an article in the newspaper. My grandfather had no fear of heights and thus came to the rescue of a young girl who was seen drowning in the Susquehanna River in the Philadelphia area. He dove into this river from an incredibly high bridge and saved her from drowning. Later in my life I came to reflect on my grandfather's life and questioned the blood that ran through his veins; I wanted to know his heritage—my heritage. I began to wonder.

You see, I was told that the Wild Bill West Show hired a lot of Native Americans. I also learned that many of the Native Americans were hired to work as steeplejack workers. They were recognized for their incredible fearlessness and a great ability to keep their balance. This was a major attribute for that job! I've been told that the reason there is a pine tree painted on the steeplejack equipment that the men climbed was that it was a tradition the American Indians started. In their tradition, they would never place themselves higher than the pine tree, or any tree, and therefore, in order for them to not stand above Mother Nature, they had the pine tree painted on top of the ladder, and they stood just one step below. It was this information, in its complexity, that led me to be very curious about my bloodline and wonder if I have a Native American ancestry. This may partially explain why I have felt such a strong draw to Native American teachings and the "calling" I feel to their lands. But what I really wonder is…*How was it, Grandfather, to date Annie???*

Ever since I was little, I have always questioned why I was here, and who created the incredible gardens in the woods and pastures. I was not raised in a religious home, but rather a great storytelling home.

I don't recall hearing the word "Spiritual" mentioned at all. However, looking back, I do remember my Pop-pop, my mother's father, coming from a warm loving heart of guidance and protection. My introduction to spirituality really came from him.

In my eyes, my grandfather was a wise man, an elder. He was a man of passion for life and he wore many hats: the farmer, the fireman, the husband, the father and the grandfather. I knew him only as "Pop-Pop." He tilled the earth and planted many seeds that bloomed into magnificent flowers, fruits, vegetables, and me — that was the farmer. He had an acre or two where he produced the fruits and vegetables our family and the neighbors would enjoy over the summer harvest. He also took care of the fire, literally and figuratively, the flame in life — that which was creative, burning within him — and that which destroyed life, threatening homes and land. When the call came, he headed to the firehouse to don the uniform and become a protector. He understood the complexity and simplicity in which we walked here on earth. Pop-pop walked in beauty. Everyone I have ever met who knew him has shared those memories of him with me.

Grandfather would take me by the hand and walk me into the garden. "Bobbie," he would say, as that was his nickname for me, "never ever pull up the vegetables underneath the earth to see if they are ready to eat. They will tell you when it is time to reap what you have sown. "

He would show me how to recognize this secret voice of Mother Nature. He loved the rain, the thunder and lightening. He recognized the great gifts held within the elements of nature as well as the dangers, therefore he taught me to have tremendous respect for these powers.

"Bobbie, let me show you how the leaves on the trees speak to us. When they turn their backs (meaning when the leaf shows its underside), we know that the wind is bringing the rain to cleanse everything."

He taught me to watch and listen to those voices that speak in silence. He knew God was in everything and shared that knowing with me in such a humble way. I did not know, when I was a very small child living with my grandparents, that I was walking on sacred ground and listening to great teachings that would one day write my myth, my story. Now, looking back, I can clearly see that so much of the way I live now had its roots in my grandfather's teachings.

My maternal grandmother was a warm loving woman who fed the entire neighborhood. Mom-Mom, as I called her, cooked up a storm. The door was always open and there was always something in the oven. Family, friends and neighbors always dropped in at Mom-Mom's house and she was always prepared. She had an open door policy: the back door was always open as well as the front. My grandparents lived near the railway that ran through the farmland. Some people would hitch a ride on railway cars — homeless travelers referred to in those days as "hobos." Word must have gotten around as they kept showing up at her back door. They were always welcomed at Grandma's. It was truly a gathering place to rest your weary soul.

I knew I could always get exactly what I wanted from Mom-Mom — when I could melt her heart.

When I was just a wee four-year-old, Mom-mom took me to buy my new holiday attire for the Easter Parade on the boardwalk, in Atlantic City. As we walked through the store, I saw exactly what was pulling me like a magnet from within. This one particular outfit spoke to me in so many ways! I was immediately connected to my intuitive nature. I knew what I wanted and what called to me, although, of course, I did not understand the depth of this calling. My eyes lit up like a wild cat's at the turquoise *leopard* outfit hanging on the rack. While I'm sure this isn't what Mom-Mom had in mind, I knew there was no turning back on this one. I grabbed it and tugged until it came off the rack and onto me. Of course, it was much too warm to wear a *leopard* outfit and never did anyone imagine a *turquoise* one at that, but I held on for dear life and Grandmother always gave in. I went home with this fabulous turquoise coat with the leopard collar — and a leopard hat adornment! This was just the beginning of my adventure with the wildness of spirit and calling to my true nature within. I loved the energy of leopard, not to mention how the turquoise felt as the color ran right through my veins, muscles, and tendons, and my skin tingled with the excitement. I looked into the mirror and realized that I had shifted right in front of my own eyes into a turquoise leopard! Can you imagine? Leopard continues to show up in my life in various ways, most especially in my dreams, but you will learn more of that as my story unfolds.

Grandfather and Grandmother were my protectors and my teachers of great wisdom. Wisdom shows up in different ways and in different forms. We need to listen for the wisdom that is shared throughout life. Through them, I have come to realize that there is a greatness in Mother Earth and she has her own story to tell, if we listen closely.

As a teenager, I discovered and explored many avenues of religious faiths. I would embrace each one with great exploration, curiosity, and faith until I felt I was caught in a box. Boxes never worked for me so when I found myself in one, I would move on to the next exploration. There were many faiths, most of them being various Christian faiths, until one day I met a delightful, very intriguing young man who embraced the Jewish faith. I was nineteen and he was twenty-two. We went on our first date August 7th and were married November 11th the same year. This was a man with great determination. Even with the great differences in our religious faiths, I agreed to the union of opposites. I was truly challenged with the idea of converting to Judaism.

This was the beginning of my entire world being turned upside down and around. I was about to enter a journey that would teach me that the *most difficult relationships were the most enlightening ones.* This partnership of marriage took me beyond what I had agreed to. As time went on I found myself living in two worlds. I converted to the Jewish faith, raised two children, a son and a daughter, in the Jewish tradition. By the time they were teenagers I felt I had completed the commitment I had agreed upon. It was time for change. My heart was pulling me in another direction. This was a time when there really was no choice but to go where the heart took me.

Chapter Two:
Opening The Box

*"Experience is not what happens to you.
It is what you do with what happens to you."*

—Aldous Huxley

After twenty years living in what I *felt* was a box, I wanted to spread my wings and explore the worlds of religion again. This was not an easy thing to accomplish when the family I embraced was living a traditional religion with very defined boundaries. Life became more of a challenge than I had bargained for, but challenges are what make us stronger.

These were the struggles that I transformed into my strengths. This did not happen overnight and there were times of great pain and heartache. I wanted to make my marriage work and struggled to find a way. When I look back at the earlier days of this struggle, I did not have the tools that I have since acquired over the past twenty years—the tools that I now share in this book. Sometimes we fail to find the bridge that can carry us over the river to the other side of understanding and awareness, or the balance where two people can walk together and meet halfway.

Finding Peace

In the struggle to find peace and make some sense of my life, I found my first tool — meditation. In meditation I developed a way of stilling the mind and finding peace that carried me through most of my day. Meditation and dreams are key tools in self-discovery. There are formal ways to meditate and there are informal ones. I read several books on meditation and also attended classes. There was also a glorious opportunity to have a formal day of meditation with a Tibetan Buddhist Nun who came to our town for several days. That was not an easy task, as I followed the instructions being given. I was told to sit straight yet be relaxed, gently soften the eyes, closed or partially closed, focus my attention between the eyes and let go of thoughts …...

There are several breath techniques that you can find in beginner's meditation guides. I recommend finding one you can relate to.

I also found other ways to meditate, like taking a walk alone in the countryside, by the ocean or in a park. I would find a quiet place that allowed me to silence the inner chatter of my mind and the outside world. Whatever it took to bring peace of mind for one moment at a time. You see, "Life is a Meditation." When we become mindful, meaning to stay present and consider where we are and what we are doing, that is Life in Active Meditation. Working with meditation was not an easy task. It took many years of patience and persistence. I was the only person in my family that meditated, so it was difficult to find that silence at home, for any length of time. The "Do not disturb" sign, when meditating, was not clearly understood. I found the solution; the time I spent soaking in the bathtub became my morning meditation time. If there is a will there is a way....

I continued to develop a meditation and yoga practice and started to enter the exploration of eastern philosophy and several modalities of healing techniques. This opened a doorway into a new world and I knew I was being guided to a place that spoke to my soul. My husband was supportive in allowing me the freedom to go and explore, and I did just that. The challenge was deciding exactly which way to go — especially since I was the only one exploring. I asked Spirit to bring joy and peace into my life and I came to realize that it comes through the process. I believed in the power of prayer and that our part is to listen to Spirit calling to us. We need to answer the phone when Spirit calls or we may miss a very important invitation. The phone I refer to is our inner knowing or communication system connected to the divine source. This is a system we need to connect to and we learn to tap into this system as we travel this journey. This communication system is available to all of us. Guess what? No charge, no bills, the system is Divine!

Watching for the Signs

I learned to hear Spirit calling and I never knew where I would be invited to go. I would hear the calling to go to many distant lands. The way I would know I was being called was through my heart. As I listened, I might feel a strong magnetic pull, or perhaps notice a sign that was given through someone or something. Listening and seeing the signposts is something that took patience and practice—as well as trust and trial. Trust is something that came from an inner feeling. I would have no solid foundation for that trust but it came from knowing that I was being led in a direction that would give my life meaning and openings for new understanding. I lived with a deep faith that a "great source," referred to by many names, God being one of them, knew what my purpose was, and I was moving in the flow of this river that changed course often. I had to watch and listen for the signs that would show up and take me by the hand, or sometimes by the seat of my pants and toss me about in order for me to move forward. These can be great wake-up calls. There were many times, I am sure, I missed the signs and went down the wrong stream "of thought," which got me into a lot of "muck" as they say!

Many times the signs are hidden in the bushes and block our vision. Well, that's when we have to look very carefully and be more curious about something that is not so obvious a sign. Start *pruning* those bushes and see what is underneath! Through time and experience I became more aware and got very curious in the adventure that waited my willingness to jump right into the river and swim without the safety of what I was comfortable with. I became stronger and knew the journey was made of my deep soul callings.

One strong call came when a dear friend introduced me to a Taoist practice. She introduced me to the teachings of "Master Mantak Chia." Spirit called and suddenly I was headed to Thailand to study with the "Master."

Following the Calling

I recall arriving in Thailand totally alone and ahead of the others that were coming to attend two weeks of meditation and Taoist training from the Master himself. I was led into the land of the unknown, waiting for whatever was going to show up; it usually did in the most unexpected ways. Upon arrival, I was stunned to realize I would be living for weeks behind a wall and gates that were constructed to keep out the wild dogs of aggression and hunger. This is not a metaphor; it is a fact. Talk about symbols in my life, this was a big one.

I was taken to my room. It was not the Ritz in which I was accustomed to residing when traveling abroad. Most of my life I had traveled a road a lot less traveled upon, but this was another *real challenge!* I had traveled across the world to arrive at a "retreat" behind bars and walls, a room that was not only not adorned with paintings, but barely painted at all. All it had in it was a small single bed, which appeared more like a cot, and a metal table and chair on which to perhaps have a cup of tea. However, this was *not my cup of tea*, as the saying goes.

Wondering what I had gotten into and whether I had misread the signs, I searched for a place of comfort and thought that a stroll on the beach with the clean fresh breeze was in order. There I would surrender all my woes to the Goddess of the Sea; this would be the solution! Not quite. When I reached the beach, no beach chairs, no beach boys, no poolside service; rather it was the day the trash was burned on the beach. This was the way of life and this was not the Boca Raton Hotel and Club, to which I was accustomed. I stood there crying, thinking that perhaps this was not the best choice of adventures, when at that moment, a hand was placed upon my shoulder and a gentle but strong voice spoke these words, "You have come here to learn a lesson that is powerful."

I turned to face a warm and loving woman standing in cutoff shorts and tee shirt. Her skin was very tan and without one added touch of ingredient upon her face, she radiated. I replied, "What if I don't learn the lesson?"

"It won't matter." She said and walked away.

She was a sign that was hard to ignore. I pondered the meaning of her words as I retreated to my "retreat."

Later into the evening hours I found myself questioning once again what I was doing at this place alone. I assumed that there were other people who had arrived and had found their way to their "lovely" abode. I apparently was the only one left awake, sitting in what appeared to be an open space resembling a lobby. I thought that perhaps I could call back home to the states and at least hold a conversation in English, since no one except the woman on the beach could speak English to me. I tried to use the telephone, but apparently by 9 P.M. the service is cut off. The women sitting behind a table did not speak English and I felt that I was about to have a panic attack, or perhaps I was already in the middle of one. At that very moment, the woman from the beach appeared next to me again. This time, she introduced herself and told me her name was Olwyn. I shared my fear and disappointment in my decision on coming there. She was such an inspiration. She helped me to feel that it was a Divine Plan that led me to this place in time. We sat and chatted girl talk for a while and than parted until morning.

It seemed that Olwyn would appear each time I was about to give up. As the days went on, I began to look for her guidance and comfort. There was a unique way she expressed her wisdom. I had recalled reading about Aborigines, the indigenous people of Australia, and I was beginning to question her heritage, as she had mentioned she was from Australia. When I presented the question to her, she hesitated, but then replied that she was Aborigine, but needed to keep her identity known only between her and I. There were others at the retreat that were from Australia and, due to the prejudice towards her heritage, she wished to avoid any judgments; I abided by her wishes even though it was difficult for me to totally comprehend the injustice that was placed upon these original people of Australia. She had been educated; not all of the culture had that advantage. With this opportunity she developed her natural skills as a visionary and the ability to turn them into beautiful stories. She entered several contests for writing and was contacted as a recipient of an award. When she appeared to accept the honor, she was denied the award. Of course, she was just told there was a mistake, that she was not actually the *chosen one*. This happened to her on more than one occasion. She was a humble woman filled with wisdom being denied her right as a writer. Today there have been some changes in the area of acceptance toward the Aborigines, but probably still not enough.

I recalled that Aborigines used the Dreamtime as a major way to move through life and process their reality. She told me that they dream everything into awareness. She told me that the earth and all its creatures had been dreamt into existence. This was a divine meeting and the two of us spent three weeks together sharing about our lives. We had become sisters!

After hours when everyone had retired to their rooms, Olwyn and I would venture to the beach. We sat under the moon and stars, and she told me about her homeland. Ularu, which is a very sacred mountain to the Aborigine, is located in the Outback. She told me how everything had a voice and a spirit. She taught me how to listen in silence to the ocean, the trees, and the land. Once again I reflected back to my childhood with my Pop-Pop and the way he helped me to be close to nature. I reflected on the turquoise leopard and how the intuitive nature of that animal called to me at the young age of four. This was the law of attraction. Olwyn would try to teach me the way of the original people (The Ancient Ones), the ancestors. They communicated through thought; there was no need for words.

"Just think something and I will know what you are asking me, "She would say."

This was way out there for me. I believed *she* could do it, but I never thought that I could ever learn to be telepathic.

"A mind reader," I said and she laughed. I sat in wonderment of it all! I was truly in the presence of a wise woman*!*

I never actually *thought* of testing her or having her *prove* her psychic abilities. She kept magically showing up just when I was about to give up; that was enough for me. It was the child in me that trusted and believed in *magic!*

Upon my return back to the states, I had wondered if the entire experience with Olwyn was all a dream. I wanted to write to her and ask her so many questions. I started to write to her and listed about ten questions I had thought of over the weeks since I had been home. I had a lot more to write about so I placed the letter into a drawer and planned to continue the letter later. Well, later turned into a lot later; I never completed the letter. Time passed and I received a letter from her. When I opened the letter and started to read, I was in amazement as Olwyn had answered all ten of my questions in the exact order that I had written them. There was no question in my mind that she knew how to *communicate in a very special way.*

Unfortunately, I have lost touch with my sister, Olwyn. She was a true friend and blessing to me.

The Hidden Lessons

She was correct when she said I had a *powerful lesson to learn!* I just had no idea that she would be the one I would learn so much from! In fact, it wasn't one powerful lesson, it was many: Sometimes the way the "signs" work is to call you somewhere thinking that you are coming for one reason (Master Chia), when in actuality the bigger impact or lesson comes as a byproduct. The original calling is often just the catalyst to get you somewhere right on time....

I realized if I let go of fear and moved on total faith, total trust, and stepped over the threshold into the unknown, I would be placed at the doorway of Divine Wisdom and Beauty.

I learned where we think we are headed is never where we land up!

I relearned to never judge a book by its cover, for you never know when a *wise woman* is undercover in a pair of cutoff shorts!.

I learned to be very careful what you dream; it may materialize.

And I learned that our thoughts and words are powerful, so think loving thoughts and speak loving words and your life will be filled with love!

I also learned that I am not separate from my brothers, my sisters, the animal kingdom and the mineral kingdom. We are creating our world and dreaming our world collectively. We dream the past, our ancestors, the present and the future.

Oh yes! Olwyn was also right when she said, "If you don't learn the lesson it will not matter." The reason being, if you don't learn it now, you can be sure it will keep showing up. Another time, another place, another form, but it will keep showing up until you do learn it!

I have reflected on that incredible experience many times over and came to realize that as the days and the three weeks progressed, I began to see the beauty in the land unfold. With an open heart and a shift in perception, I came to see beauty in what was surrounding me in all directions. There is great wonder and magic afoot when you begin to journey where you have never ventured before — and when you can see beauty in a place where at first it eluded you. This is when you truly step out of the box. Some adventures in life can be frightening, challenging, and a door presenting a new world of possibilities…if we are willing to take the step through that doorway.

Meditate and Visualize:

Find a comfortable place to sit. You may want to play soft music in order to relax into a calm and peaceful state. Take a few deep breaths and release the tension held in your body. Now, think of something that may feel impossible to do or complete, then visualize a doorway opening to the other side. When you walk through this doorway you will enter a space where all possibilities exist. See your greatest passion or desire you wish to achieve fulfilled. Feel it, sense it, hold it in your heart. Use all your senses to make this real in all ways. Know that the magic is within you...You hold the key! Take a moment to send gratitude to Source for recognizing this achievement.

Notes

_____

_____

_____

_____

_____

_____

_____

_____

_____

_____

_____

_____

_____

_____

_____

_____

_____

_____

_____

_____

_____

_____

_____

_____

Chapter Three:
Two Worlds

"Go confidently in the direction of your dreams.
Live the life you have imagined."

—Henry David Thoreau

It was hard to leave home and sometimes even harder to return, depending upon the adventure and assignment that spirit gave me. I would return from my adventures with such excitement, wild experiences, new teachings to share and a heart overflowing with stories to tell. I expected my family to see and feel the messages that were packed into the adventure. It was difficult for them to understand my enthusiasm over the challenges I had incurred, but I would still try to convince them that there was great wisdom and knowledge held within the story and teachings I would share. I seemed to be the only one getting the message. At times, it seemed they would have a good laugh at my expense, never seeing all the wisdom that was hidden within the metaphor and symbolism of my encounters. Perhaps the messages were only meant for me, but I am sure we can all relate on some level to experiencing those things in life that make our hearts sing and wanting our loved ones to sing and dance along with us.

When our songs are not heard and our dance is not recognized, do we give up on listening to our Soul's call? No! Never give up on your spiritual quest! If we cannot take our loved ones along on our journey, we still must continue to follow our souls' calling. Persistence, trust, faith, and knowing there is a bigger plan waiting to be revealed to us at some later date, helps us to keep on keeping on!

I ask myself today, where have the stories gone? Have we forgotten to share our stories and listen deeply from the heart? We need to go back, only to remember, that the stories have a piece of each of us in them. How can we be present for each other? What is hidden beneath our busy days and hurried lives that needs to be brought into the light? Today I would say to my children and grandchildren; tell your stories and your dreams. If you do not have a circle of family or friends to share your story, then a journal can become your most precious friend as a place to write your stories.

As time went on, I found myself with two homes — one on the east coast in Boca Raton, Florida with my husband, and one on the west coast in Orange County, California, alone. Life was a dichotomy. I somehow had the idea or illusion that I could live in both worlds. I went on believing that for seven years as I traveled back and forth month after month, week after week. The journey never got easier and the returning home got more difficult. I then started to question which of the returns was actually "The return home."

I began to look at the questions, "How do I live in two worlds, and what are the two worlds?" What I came to realize was that the two worlds were the physical/material world and the spiritual world. These two worlds were separate. On the east coat, I lived a life filled with all the luxury, comfort, and security. The west coast was a place where I was free to embrace my spiritual life and live my dream. I was living in two worlds, both physically and figuratively, and somehow there was no bridge that connected the two.

Well, the west kept calling, Spirit kept calling, and one day I answered the call. I packed my bags and returned to the one place where I could live life fully, from the inside out.

This returning home did not come by an easy route — no way! It was with tears, grief, questioning and tremendous heartbreak. I desperately wanted my partner to come with me. As I have shared already and will perhaps mention again, we cannot always take those we love with us. They have their choices to make and their lives to live and perhaps the two lives no longer meet at the same doorway. Sometimes I wonder, did they ever meet there? I have given great hours, days, weeks, months and quite a few years to contemplating that understanding. It took seven years of unraveling the threads that had bound me and to weave the tapestry of my life, revealing a greater vision, before I could come to peace in my heart on the choice I had made. Sometimes we don't make the choice; the choice is made for us way before we come to that realization.

How do we begin to live from the inside out? I needed to go deep into that place inside where I had old beliefs and programs that told me there were two worlds. Since my partner and I shared different beliefs in religion and the way we saw our daily inspirations, desires and wishes played out, I believed there were two different worlds. There is only one world and it expands and moves in glorious ways when we learn how to integrate our feelings, our desires, our creativity, and our actions in the world, with a loving, understanding heart. In this way we can share together what each of us holds dear. It allows expansion, not separation. As I followed my dreams and nightmares, I started to see where I had separated the two. This did not happen quickly. It took months and years of following my dreams, meditating, reflecting and being willing to go into the dark uncharted waters of denial. I had to see where my vision was clouded over. I came to realize I lived in places of illusion. My perception only allowed me to see where my awareness was at that moment. We can never see where we are until we move forward and look back. I took the time to look back, but not in regret, only to see the growth that came out of my willingness to enter those painful places.

We have all heard the expression, "money is the root of all evil," but that is true only if we are attached to it. It has taken me years to understand the meaning of attachment. It was like peeling an onion layer by layer. Many tears were shed as my attachments were ripped away. I wanted to hold on and not let go of all the comforts and *things* I had gathered along the way. I had to surrender and trust I would be given all I needed to be peaceful, happy and joyful. Underneath the layers of the onionskin was a new vision of self. Through my experiences, my trials and errors, I came to live more from the inside. This is something hard to understand; only personal experiences can bring us to this place. I began to see my outer world changing, even in the friends I attracted to myself and the activities in which I became engaged. As the inside was deeply looked into, my outer world was changing. We can read, gather greater understanding and knowledge, however, it is through the experiences of life that *wisdom blossoms.*

Diving Into Trust

Over and over I questioned my life and where I stood. My trust and willingness to step into the unknown over and over brought me to the place I stand today in greater understanding and joy. I had to be willing to walk through doors that seemed to go nowhere, yet on the other side was a new horizon, new experiences that inspired me to continue. There were times that I felt I had made mistakes, but as we may have heard before, *there are no mistakes, only teachings!* I try to always remember that statement as it helps me not to go into regret and guilt. You see, I know from experience that regret and guilt are blocks on our path to our unfolding and to reaching a greater place to stand and experience God.

I have come to realize that I have not written this story, the story is writing me, and continues to do so. Isn't that the way, when we stop to think about our lives — are we writing our myth or is the myth writing us? I have given that some thought and come to find that the myth writes me, but I have come to *write the pages of my life.* I have to put into place those experiences of my life and bring them into a new light! I reflect on the past only to bring it into new understanding.

Keep journaling…

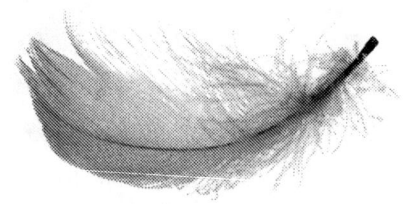

Question to meditate upon:

Does the ground that you stand on support your life fully? This does not mean the literal Earth; it touches deeper into a place in the Soul. Does it resonate with what is calling you from inside your heart, where you can live fully and shine your light in the outer world? Are you living from the inside out? This may be something you wish to journal over a period of days, weeks or even months. Give yourself permission to ask for those things that make your heart sing. Ask for the support you need to stand your ground. Keep dreaming it forth.

Notes

_____

_____

_____

_____

_____

_____

_____

_____

_____

_____

_____

_____

_____

_____

_____

_____

_____

_____

_____

_____

_____

_____

_____

_____

_____

Chapter Four:
Messages Come in Many Forms

"I can never decide whether my dreams are the result of
my thoughts,
or my thoughts the results of my dreams."

-D.H. Lawrence

At one point in our marriage, my husband gave me a very special gift, a beautiful Native American Indian-crafted necklace. This necklace held a knowing, a vibration, a spirit that led me to a place where I would be taught to 'walk in beauty.' This precious gift had a secret inside. However, until it was broken open, the message would be kept hidden.

One day this priceless necklace fell from my hand onto a tile floor, cracked and broke open. I had tried many times to have this necklace repaired; there was never anyone that was willing or able to repair the broken pieces. There were many times when it was suggested that I simply replace it with something new and more up-to-date. I had a very difficult time with replacement and was attached to it on many levels. I knew this necklace held a story.

I put it away, until one day I met someone who knew the exact person, a Hopi Indian, who would repair this piece and allow the story to be told. *Our stories must be told.* Everything has a voice and a spirit. I always knew that I would be willing to pay any price to have it mended. Little did I know how the pieces would mend many lives, and what the price would be. I sent it off with high hopes of restoration.

A few months later, a package arrived. With great anticipation and excitement to see the silver and all the beauty of the precious stones, coral, lapis and turquoise, I carefully unwrapped the package containing the necklace restored to its wholeness, to its perfect beauty. Inside was a note written by the hand that preciously tended to the mending of the broken pieces, *"There are some things in life that can not have a price placed onto them."* I had not been charged for the necklace's repair. I sat there with a precious necklace in one hand and a precious note in the other, unable to tell in that moment which was more valuable. I had been given a gift with no idea or understanding of the many, many gifts that would come from this first mending. I knew at once the greatness of the Soul that gave this back in its wholeness; it was someone connected to a greater power of love beyond my understanding at that moment in time. In this wound came a gift that was beyond anything I could have imagined! The gift came from the hands that had mended the necklace and made it whole once more. Those hands and heart live a life of walking in beauty, and over the years has became a mentor and beloved friend. He has helped mend my broken heart many times over. In many ways, he has made me whole once more, as well. Today, we share dreams and the mysteries of life that unfold as we surrender each day to Spirit.

The Medicine Inside the Wound

I am blessed to have Benny and his lovely wife as my friends. Benny continues to mentor me in the ways of understanding Spirit and the gifts that were hidden beneath my fears, pain and guilt. I was told that those emotions were blocks to my journey on this path called life. He has guided me to realizing that we all have a journey and that I may journey down a different path than my loved one, but that each of these paths come to the one place where the *one source* lives within each of us.

This is how I found my life to unfold many times over. Through heartbreak and disappointment came new wonders of love and joy. *It's always in the cracking open, that the greater gift is revealed.* There were many times in my life where I did not see these heartbreaks as gifts. When feeling despair and traumatized, I only saw the door slamming closed, but when I surrendered to the Divine Power I knew existed, doorways opened into new worlds of exploration and even greater love. Once I recognized that gift, it was easier to move through pain, sadness and deep grief. I began to recognize that the medicine was hidden within the wound. I needed to surrender each time to the alchemy of the potion.

There were many compromises in life when I stepped over the boundaries onto new land of daring adventure and living my dream. This was a time that allowed my expression to flow as the river and began to bring the balance of heaven and earth into realization. I had to learn to move through life in a different way. The first thing that was exchanged was the way I got around. You see, in Boca Raton I traveled around in a beautiful Black Jaguar. That car had to be left behind, however; hidden within that wound was another wonderful gift — a wonderful four-wheel drive Land Rover. Now that got me all over the USA; it gave me the wheels to roam the land. I ventured into the mountains and rivers of the four corners of the United States where the Native American Culture had thrived.

Animal Messengers

I came to a land where the Shaman and Medicine Man still lived. I had come to answer the call of the mountain and found a land filled with my secret yearnings. This is the land where my soul called to me. Here was the place I came to experience nature. I came to a place that stirred deep within me that four-year-old child that had become The Turquoise Leopard. I now got to know the instinctual nature that lived within me; I came to recognize the animal spirit guides that would show up throughout my life in dreamtime and waking life. I started to pay close attention when any and all of the animals and birds entered my space. There are great teachings to learn from the creatures of the earth. I moved inside the wild passion of life and I became more curious about the jaguar that lived within me — the one I rode instead of drove.

The way of the Shaman was to embody the energy and learn from its nature. Jaguar and other cats repeatedly roamed through the landscape of my dreams. These cats belonged to a family called the Leopard, and included the Jaguar and Panther. I researched the nature of these cats that came to visit in my dreams and, with that knowledge, gained a greater understanding of myself and what was being shown to me through my animal spirit guides. I honor those that visit in dreams and visions and allow them to lead the way. I became more curious and quietly observed their presence. I began to recognize the dream had several messages. One message was for the personal self and another message was holding the bigger picture that nature is calling to awaken the world. Our dreams may be bringing us messages that are a call from the wild and our earth. We continue to invade the land where animal life thrives. We continue to make concrete jungles. We pollute the water and air. We move deeper into the wildlife, remove the land where fauna and flora thrive, in order to create highways and toll roads for our convenience. We label this progress; is it? Where is the green earth that once supported all of us. The next time a lion, bobcat, whale or dolphin enters your nighttime voyage, or even shows up in your awaking dream, ask the question, why am I receiving this call? What is the symbolic message for me? What is the bigger picture for the collective? It may just be for you personally, but remember, we are all connected.

I wanted to explore the Native Land and listen to the voice of the Ancestors. My soul yearned to find more of the answers that lingered in my heart from childhood. I continued to ask Spirit to guide me and lead to the place of understanding.

I wish to share more about the animals that come to visit in dreamtime and sometimes in my waking visions. Some people may call this their great imagination. I know from experience that without imagination I could not bring into the world many of the dreams that I dream. Isn't that the way of the inventor? How often did great ideas come in dreams to those who could see through the dream?

When I lived in Florida I had a dream. I was listening to one of my favorite drumming CD's, as the music of the drum began to beat with my heart, the rhythm took me deeper and deeper into another land. *I traveled down a waterfall into a deep cave into the earth; I was face to face with a very large jaguar. Brilliant emerald green eyes starred into my clear sky blue eyes. I did not turn in fear, for jaguar knew me as I knew her; then our souls met. She turned and I climbed upon her back; she moved forward and suddenly, but gently, my right arm and shoulder melted into hers. Then my left arm and shoulder became one with hers. Then my right leg moved into her, followed by the left leg. Our bodies became one as I began to see through the brilliant green eyes of jaguar. I roamed the land and felt the earth in a way I had never felt before. I saw the trees from the earth floor and knew the roots beneath my feet,* moving instinctually and feeling all life surrounding me. I was given a New Vision, a New World. I became the dream or, in other words, I embodied the dream. The dream was moving in my vibrational body and something shifted. I was awakened.

That was my first of several dreams over the years where the family of large cats joined my world, or I joined theirs. You could say they awakened me to awareness of nature and how we are all one within it. Our personal dream and the world are not separate. I continue to remember to connect with Mother Earth and listen to her cries and calls. She lives and breathes us — we live life as one. What we feed her — she feeds us!

I know there was a time I did not realize that everything lives and breathes as we do. When I need to remember, I call on jaguar to take me on a journey — when I need to feel what is beating with the great life force. If we listen to the creatures of the earth and air, we can find a connection greater than ourselves.

Where the messages will come from, and who or what the messengers are, isn't always clear. As you venture into the world of dreams and visions, remember, the world is *alive* and dreaming with us and within us. Dreams are a great form of medicine. As we heal ourselves, we heal the world. Sometimes, oddly enough, things have to break for a healing to take place. Navigating the river of dreams — and dream messages — is a great form of listening and awareness.

I invite you on the journey with me.

Meditation:

Take one of your favorite CD's, or perhaps even try something new and adventuresome!

Sit in a comfortable chair or lie down on the floor with some cozy blankets.

Find a place that feels safe and comfortable.

Begin to slowly take a few deep breaths; let the breath out slowly and relax into the vibration of the sound. Allow the vibrations to flow through your body.

Allow whatever comes to your mind to take you on an adventure.

Explore where you have never dared to go before. Just let whatever comes move you into a deeper sense of being completely there, completely present in the moment.

Be inquisitive. For example, if a color shows up in your vision, feel the vibration of that color. Try to feel what it would be like to actually be that color. If an animal appears, look into its eyes, follow it and see where it wants to take you, or what it has to show you. Be curious and investigate dreamtime. Here, in a slightly altered state, you can journey and move about in the field of dreams.

When you are complete and feel ready to journey back, start to breathe deeply and take your time for your re-entry. Come back to a total awareness of where you are and be present in the room once again.

Take your journal and write what you have experienced. You may find this to be a new way to explore places inside yourself that you never ventured to know before.

Notes

_____

_____

_____

_____

_____

_____

_____

_____

_____

_____

_____

_____

_____

_____

_____

_____

_____

_____

_____

_____

_____

_____

_____

_____

_____

Chapter Five:
The Heartbeat Of The Mountain Called To Me

*"Alone and without its nest must the eagle fly
across the face of the sun."*

—*Kahlil Gibran*

I continue to hear the callings and I continue to answer.

One time I was called to Canyon De Chelly and the ancient ruins of the Anasazi Indians. This was a time in my life when I wanted to use my creative eye in photography. I had developed a very close relationship with the world of photography. My teacher became my dear friend and explorer in the Indian Territory where we ventured into the canyons with his associates. This was a great adventure and a time for me to really explore the mountains, cliffs and caves. I was very excited and, yes, there was the challenge of a little danger involved. Climbing up and down the ropes to the fatal cliffs and vistas of the Anasazi ruins was no small feat for me, especially with a backpack full of camera equipment! Spirit may call, but does not tell us what we need to carry! These were incredible places where the Spirit of the Ancient Ones still walked upon the earth; I could sense their presence. There is much to respect and honor when walking Sacred Ground. There were many times that I would put my camera equipment down and just listen.

There was a dream I had one time, many years prior to this journey to this land of the Native American Indian. The *dream* spoke to me and said, "*Voices that hear.*" This was one of those dreams that I had to be patient with, very patient. My dream began to make sense, many years later, as this was the place where the voices spoke to me in the silence.

There were many ruins to venture into; however, there were two that especially called to me. The first one was Eagle's Nest, and that was the most daring and dangerous. This was one climb I decided not to take, at first. The height was more than I could imagine climbing and, to top it all off, there was barely a ledge to step onto when you got to the top. As I watched the others, it was so frightening to witness their incredible desire to reach Eagle's Nest that it took strength just to watch the climb and hold onto the rope from the bottom, supporting their safety so each of them could be successful. Wow, I certainly respected those that had the courage to go for it! After they returned, we moved on to another dwelling, which gave us more solid, safer ground beneath our feet. The Eagle kept calling, however, and I finally left the group to venture back toward Eagle's Nest. I felt totally alone as I walked back toward the cliff, but then I realized, I'm not alone; Spirit was at my side. I have been told by many of my guides and mentors that Spirit is always with us, but sometimes I forget. We continue to be human and fall into the forgetfulness of thinking we are alone.

As I walked, I felt someone trailing behind me; it was a woman from the group coming to find out where I was headed and to check on my safety. She had no idea how grateful I was to see her coming with me. Of course, I did not want to show the fear that accompanied my outrageous adventuresome nature. Well, we arrived and there it was—that climb to the heavens above. That is what it surely felt like to me.

She asked if I wanted to venture first and I replied, "Oh no, you go ahead and I'll stable the rope ladder." Always being the stabilizing force for others, I never even thought about no one being left to stabilize the rope for me.

I wanted to wait so I could gather up a little more courage. I observed her every step, as well as her strength, for she was half my age. Suddenly I said to myself, do not limit yourself because of a number connected to the years of experience you have had here on this earth. It was my turn to climb and to meet the challenge. I grabbed tightly with my hands and then tighter and tighter, until they began to feel as if I would rub them raw with each move and each step I took. It was Autumn, but it felt like the middle of summer the way I was sweating — both from the effort and from the fear of falling. I then got a grip on the entire matter and remembered the advice I had once heard, "Never look back from where you came." That was a good thing to remember half way up the climb. My friend told me that the view was so amazing that I would not believe it, so, with just a few more steps to climb, I gritted my teeth and a hand reached down to pull me onto the very edge of the cliff.

"Stay on your hands and knees," she called, "Since there is very little room to move about and stand safely."

I kissed the stone where I placed my hands and knees. I had landed on Eagle's Nest! I placed a gift in one of the crevices of the cliff dwelling. It was a special crystal I had carried to be left as a gift to the mountain and Spirit. I sat for a few moments to give thanks for my safety, to realize the heights that I had climbed – literally and figuratively

— and the strong pull from my heart to reach a place where the Ancestors lived in the most brutal weather and under the sparsest of conditions. I took the time to ponder their lives and the abundance and gifts of life that I have. These were the people that took *the road less traveled and cut the pathway for our feet to walk today.*

Then it was time for the climb back down. If you think the climb up was something, try going in reverse. I had been warned before about climbing mountains. "It's not the climb up that is the most dangerous; it is the climb back down." Well, again I grabbed the rope as tight as I could and started in reverse. You know that feeling that you want to look around and see where you are? Well, not this time. I did not want to see where I could end up — which was thousands of feet into a ravine that certainly was a killer. One step at a time or should I say — one piece of rope at a time. When my feet touched the earth, I felt like I had traveled a lifetime in just one hour. I was ready for more solid ground under my feet for the rest of the day, but was joyful that I had answered the Eagle's call.

Next, we went to a place called *She House*. When this ruin was originally discovered, they found that one of the dwellings held the remains of an ancestor of the days gone by. She was the only one found within the ruin. There was a Kiva within this dwelling. A Kiva is a sacred place where the men would go and pray. They are built beneath the level of earth. They were not always deep, and most times you had to crawl down on you hands and knees, unable to stand up. I asked if I could go down into the Kiva. Our guide told me that it generally was not a custom to allow anyone in the Kiva, however, she told me she would allow me to do this if I respected the Sacred Space. She made it clear that she would not take any responsibility for any danger that could occur. I understood and took responsibility for what I was about to do.

I honored the land and the Ancestors' home and knew that I would need permission to enter the dwelling from *them*, not just our guide. I asked the Ancestors, those that once lived on this land, with a prayerful voice. I asked them from the voice of my heart. I told them that I was a white woman who honored their traditions and felt the calling of their land strong within me. I longed to know Spirit from their hearts and asked if I could enter their dwelling place of prayer. Suddenly, I was being pulled by a force greater than myself. This force pulled me into the Kiva and I knew they had answered.

THE VOICES THAT HEAR

I sit quietly, sensing the presence of the ancient spirits
who have gone before me.

My soul knows that they are watching and listening.

I ask that I may honor their presence
and enter their holy dwelling.

I wait for the Answer
as my strength holds me still.

My Answer is revealed in my heart,
and the understanding from the Ancient ones
pulls me forth to enter their dwelling.

Peace flows through me and I feel their presence.
Their voices speak to me of Great Spirit.

Never a doubt in the hearts and minds of truth.

Great Spirit is in the land.
Great Spirit blossoms in the flower.

Great Spirit flows through the river,
and is the strength of the mountains.

Great Spirit moves as the wind
and warms us by the sun,

She cools us by the Moon
and nurtures us through the mother.

Great Spirit blesses us with each breath we take.

The Ancient ones whispered to me of this great gift
and I give thanks to the Voices that Hear.

In the stillness of nature I allowed the voice to be heard. When I listened closely, I realized that there is a voice to be heard *within* me, *my inner voice!* I started to listen and placed those words onto pages that created many journals.

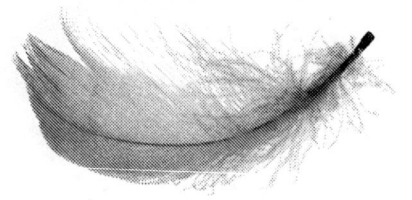

Creative writing
experience

Find a place in nature to relax. It can be in your own garden or some special place you like to go. Open your heart and mind to whatever speaks to you. When you are ready, take your journal and pen; begin to write whatever comes to you. The flowers, trees, birds, or an animal may speak to you in your inner silence. Like a child, tell a story. Do not edit or be concerned how it may sound. Your creative child has a story to tell. There may even be an ancestor that has a story to tell through your voice.

Notes

_____

_____

_____

_____

_____

_____

_____

_____

_____

_____

_____

_____

_____

_____

_____

_____

_____

_____

_____

_____

_____

_____

_____

_____

_____

_____

_____

_____

Part 2:
Dream Messengers Waking and Asleep

"Our truest life is when we are in our dreams awake."

—Henry David Thoreau

Chapter Six: Unpacking The Emotions

"And the day came when the risk to remain tight in a bud was more painful than the risk it took to blossom."

—Anaïs Nin

As you may have realized by now, I am a person with a curious and adventuresome nature. I have climbed many mountains, from America to the Himalayas in Nepal. I also climb "the mountain" in metaphor. When we tend our dreams, we can climb many peaks, but first, unlike a normal trip for which we *pack* our things, for our spiritual journey we must *unpack* our metaphorical "suitcases."

I realized, at some point in my life, that I could not take my Louis Vuitton trunk up Mt. Everest. Now *that* is a metaphor. You see, as we climb to higher peaks of awareness and embrace the crystal clear vision of greater understanding, we must let go of those things that weigh us down and make our journey *up the mountain to Spirit* difficult. We cannot climb the mountain with all that luggage upon our backs, dragging our trunks with us! These heavy loads are the roadblocks to the top. I know for myself that the more I let go, the faster I can climb.

I also know that whoever my partner is in life, he must also carry a 'light' load; perhaps to climb this mountain together, we shall only travel with a backpack.

So, let's try this journey to the top of the mountain; let's lighten our load. You can either start the climb without all your baggage, or just let it go one piece at a time. You will come to realize the *unpacking* is the journey; *the choice of what you wish to carry is up to you! Journaling my dreams and emotions* has been the greatest tool I could have been given to look closely at what I am carrying that weighs me down and help me to unpack my luggage.

I have been unpacking for years. Here is how it has worked for me:

I have the small backpack on for my next journey; it hasn't always been small but after a lot of journaling, dream work, meditating and crying as a release of the past, I have gotten the "load" down to a manageable size. I may still be "carrying" an issue with my daughter that I need to resolve, or an incident with my former spouse or my neighbor that I need to release, but mostly within my backpack now, I carry my tools for processing the situations that arrive in my life. I have carefully chosen to carry courage. I have carefully chosen to carry — at all times — a journal and a pen. These items are weightless because they help me "unpack" the emotions that may arise throughout my day. But then, somewhere along the way something may happen and I forget to get out the tools that I know I have available to me for resolving whatever I am facing. Instead, I decide to gather some more items along the way — maybe I add a little hurt from a comment someone said, or a pound or two of fear over finances, or a brick or two of judgment about the way a family member or friend is handling a situation, or anger over an injustice I feel has been done to me. These items are not carefully chosen, but unconsciously added to my load.

The burden starts to affect my balance and my breathing. Now, if you look at this literally and as a metaphor, you can see we must keep looking deep into the things that we hold on to and those things that catch us off guard. There are times when we need to stop; take a few deep breaths, and come back to center. When we come back to center, we are coming back to the peace and strength that is the foundation we build upon. When we are centered, we can take a moment to set the "backpack" down, look inside to see what is throwing us off balance or weighing us down, and literally unpack the baggage. Using the tools of journaling, dream work, metaphor and meditation will help you to either let go of the baggage or, *by Grace,* it may simply disappear. Often, it is just a new perspective that makes an issue simply dissolve. A moment of compassion, understanding or empathy for someone else can, in a heartbeat, cause an issue to go away. Asking for that which I need to see, always yields a message that is valuable.

Relationships also show up to mirror what we cannot see. All relationships are sacred and valuable as they guide us to greater understanding and, *like* a *dream,* can reflect the greater development of the self. Just as the dream can reflect that which we neglect to see in waking state, our relationships can be the mirror for us to see clearly, the shadow (aspects we can't see) within. This gives us another opportunity to unpack once again.

The Gift of Journaling

Journaling can serve many forms of expression; my journals are my voice — my heart and soul brought into form. I am taking the liberty here of changing the noun of "journal" into the verb of "journaling," meaning "writing in your journal." Here, I am going to share with you many of the ways that I have used journaling on my own journey — to unpack my bags and to make sense of my life. I invite you to explore these methods with your own writing.

Expressive Journaling

Often, I use my journal to unpack my emotions by expressing my thoughts and feelings on paper in whatever way they wish to be expressed. I do not worry about the correct form when I write, for I write exactly what I feel. I do not judge or edit what I feel. Sometimes the words come from great sadness, pain, grief or anger, and other times from great joy, excitement and passion. Sometimes my feelings are expressed through writing poetry, prose or stories. I realize I have a poetic voice, a gift I have recognized through journaling. Pen to paper, I say!

With Wings To Fly was written at a time when I was torn with sadness and grief about leaving my marriage, and making my journey alone as a single woman.

WITH WINGS TO FLY

I have wings to fly, but first I walked. The door has opened to walk the path. I hesitated knowing the pain that touches each step on the path made of stones. I look and see their pointed and jagged edges that move up into my life. I feel the road with all the life and the texture that I am to become. Along this path is the hidden beauty of the smooth silky stones that have been made to step on and feel the loving comfort within. They have stood the turbulent waves of the ocean; the trodden ways gave them their smoothness of life. They send love and healing through my being.

*I take the first step and hesitatingly place my bare exposed foot onto
the first rock. It embraces me with its edge. It releases the memory
of pain and transmutes down into Mother Earth. As I realize this
journey will teach me to heal myself, I ask for courage and strength
to embrace all the stones on the path. I look up and see a light that
shines so bright that the stones become golden in the glow, My heart
tells me that many steps will be broken with sharp edges that will
cause great pain. I know the beauty at the end of the path is in
knowing that the walk healed all the sorrow of many life times. I
know, as I place one foot in front of the other, my journey is guided
by God. There is someone at my side holding my hand, someone in the
front leading the way, and someone behind me gently placing a hand
on my shoulder, steering me forward with loving care. He is all three
and we are one. I know I am safe; my bare feet will endure all that
is beneath them. I know that my heart will lead me to other worlds
beyond my feet and I will have WINGS TO FLY!*

———————————

There were times my heart would cry tears that flowed as words
upon the paper. As the words appeared, my heart began to release
something I did not understand at that time. I always say, we must be
patient for the understanding is not always present in the moment of
surrender. I would read the words that flowed from my broken heart,
many times, each time realizing a new vision for myself. Understanding
one's own healing journey is often similar to interpreting a dream; the
depth of understanding keeps unfolding. I came to realize that my life
was like a flower that was opening, I just needed to remember to water
and fertilize it with love and care.

My very first Buddhist teacher was Thich Nhat Han. I met him
in Santa Barbara, California, and spent five days of silent retreat along
with the wisdom teachings he so lovingly shared. He speaks and writes

often about us blooming as a flower. This is a quote from his book on anger:

"You may think that you have to combat evil and chase it out of your heart and mind. But, this is wrong. The practice is to transform yourself. If you don't have garbage, you have nothing to use in order to make compost, you have nothing to nourish the flower in you.

"Both our negative feelings and positive feelings are organic and belong to the same reality.

"She had many wonderful seeds in her, but her husband had not recognized them. He had not watered them. He had watered only her negative seeds because he did not practice."

"If you had really practiced watering the positive seeds in your beloved, than he or she would not cause you so much suffering today. So you are partly responsible for your suffering."

The challenges and suffering we go through in our life are necessary so we have that sustenance to transform them into our strengths. I know that these have been the things that have given me opportunities to transform and become the stronger woman I am today. I continue to remember his words; many times I fall down and need to pick myself up and start to water the seeds once again. "Barbara, Barbara, quite contrary, *how does your garden grow?"* With much love and care-full tending! I need to remember to *weed the garden, also.*

Sometimes powerful journaling can be inspired by a passage such as this, that allows you to look at yourself and your circumstances in a new way. By writing about them, new insights emerge that you might have missed entirely. When we make sense of the things that have happened to us and take responsibility for our part in the creation of our suffering, we unpack the emotions surrounded an event, and we are better able to lay them down so we no longer have to carry them.

Mending Emotions

Journaling has been a great way to process my emotions, allowing me to let them go. Many times the pain or grief was so deep that until I took the pen in hand I did not know where to go or what to do with the feeling. Once the feelings were expressed, they seemed to dissipate, and light would shine upon a greater understanding and a new perception would evolve from the process.

For many years throughout my marriage, I had collected these very precious teapots. I had been given several of them from my daughter, friends and aunt. I used them often and kept them on a shelf for everyone to enjoy their beauty when they were not serving my guests with delightful teas. I never kept them stored away, as I wanted to share the love and beauty they expressed.

When I moved from Florida to California, I requested that my husband send the teapots. I felt they would be safe, since I had many other precious, fragile items, shipped previously. One afternoon, I arrived home to find the package at my door. Very excited with great anticipation to see my precious teapots and place them on a shelf in my new home, I proceeded to open the box. I found they had not been carefully wrapped nor was it even mentioned on the outside of the box that there were fragile items inside. My beautiful collection was in hundreds of pieces. I cried bitterly for the loss of my treasures. I cried for loss of my past. I cried for loss of care and concern that my husband and I once shared. I sobbed and sobbed and then picked up a pen and paper to write my grief into expression. At that point, I realized that I was holding onto the past. The journaling that came from that grief was this poem. When the last word was written, the tears had stopped and I felt the peace within.

Fading Memories

*We try to hold on to the beauty of the past in doing so the
pain is woven as a web that entraps the movement and
expansion.*

*It comes in shattered bits and pieces and lies upon
our door post and Hearts in sorrow.*

*For what has been broken cannot be mended into perfection;
If mended, cannot be used in its strength,
for the crack remains to show its fragile existence.*

*Like beautiful porcelain, life must be treasured and tendered
with love, for in a moment's touch it fades into non-existence.
We shall not pour our Hearts from broken vessels,
only the fading memories.*

———————

I wrote these thoughts in my journal: How do we hold that which is precious to someone else when we do not know or understand what lies inside unseen? How do we hold that which belongs to another? How do we acknowledge, in an understanding way, something that is important and cherished by another? We may not understand why, but we can honor what they hold dear and try our best to keep it safe. That is what relationship is about. Relationship with our beloved partner, our brothers, sisters, our neighbors and all those we see and touch. What we hold onto can be illusions, yet other times they are treasured memories.

This was a lesson on letting go. Letting go continues throughout time and brings greater awareness into our lives.

I continually look at the metaphors in my daily life. The metaphor I saw in the broken pieces of those cherished teapots was about *picking up the pieces.* I explored the metaphor of something that I had cherished within the journey of my marriage coming to me in many broken pieces. The pieces of the teapots represented all the moments that were treasured during my thirty-five years of marriage. I felt my *life* shattered into those pieces. Life is like precious porcelain and must be handled with care — and it hadn't been. Now, I had to reach down and pick up each piece and try to put it all back together — literally and figuratively. *Where would I begin?* As the writing says, *if it could be mended the crack would always be there.* I knew I had to start over and let go of the things that could not be mended. There were only memories that could be cherished and treasured; that is an important understanding when we move on and pick up the pieces.

Now was the time to let go and move forward in creating new joy and new memories that would be the beginning of my new life as a single woman. These were not easy times that lay ahead; I continued to struggle without knowing what my future held. This was a place of total trust and faith; I was being guided to a new vision. I needed to rely on a strong foundation in a power greater than I. There were times I questioned Spirit regarding the loneliness, grief and pain that I lived with throughout each day. My meditations and prayers were a great tool and comfort in helping me with this. I knew that it was important to feel the pain and keep moving through it. I learned not to stay in those places of great sadness for long periods of time. I was blessed with a support system of wonderful friends and mentors and had tremendous trust that what I did not understand would one day be revealed to me. This was a time that taught me great patience. I have found when things happen in my life that are either distressing or out of the norm, if I take a step back and look at them as if they are a dream, I gain a different perspective that allows me to find the message, or the lesson. If I had looked at the tea pots as just a life event, I would have simply gotten angry, and would not have been able to see the metaphors of picking up the pieces and letting go of that which can not be mended.

Dream Journaling

A journal is a valuable tool for both recording and making sense of dreams —sleeping *and* waking dreams. Dream journaling is my passion and my daily practice. This is the record of my nighttime journey. I could also say it is my nighttime job, as it is what has changed the way I see the world and move within it daily. I keep my journal and pen by my bedside wherever I travel. I am never without it. I never want to miss an important message or insight that may suddenly shift my perception. I write everything down from my dreams. It can be words that I hear or written signs that I see. There can be colors, voices, emotions, bits and pieces that make no sense, but I write them down. You see, you never know when the answers from your dream will appear in your waking life. It must be written down as soon as you awaken. Dreams will quickly leave your mind as soon as you answer the phone or start heading towards that shower in the morning. Oh yes, the mind does play tricks on us, especially when we think the dream was so incredible that we shall never forget *this* one. Well, just wait and see, you *will* forget!

Then there are times we think we remember exactly how the dream has unfolded but the mind moves in mysterious ways. Your mind will change the message if you don't write it down exactly as it happened right away. Try it out: write down a dream and then weeks later try to explain the dream in detail to a friend. Then check what was written for accuracy. You will see how our minds work to deceive us!

One of my favorite things to do is to ask a question before I go to bed. I write the question into my dream journal and date it. Then, I allow the answer to unfold in my dreams. Here is an example of one of my question and answer dreams.

Date June 8, 2004

Question: Tell me the best way to write my book!

Dream: First there was a verbal message: *"Allow Spirit to speak through you, the words will come — you are a painter of words."*

Then, the visual dream starts to appear — with me in it. *I am given a paintbrush. I place the first stroke of color upon the canvas and I feel the creative expression with me. The dream comes alive and I become the writer, the actor, director and audience. The dream shifts and the stage is reset — a new canvas to paint.*

I wake up!

In this dream I received a message in answer to my question. The first part of the dream with the voice speaking to me held the answer. The rest of the dream told me that writing my book would be my creative expression. Our lives are our canvases that we create and write. We are the actor, the director of our lives, and as we look upon our experiences, we become the audience. Do we like what we see? Well, if not, let's change it! We can ask for help there also. We can ask for anything. *But, we must be patient*; it takes time to perfect anything. Don't give up on the process.

Dream Messages

As I shared above, before I go to bed I ask for guidance in the form of *a dream or image* that will show me what it is that I am holding onto. *What is it that blocks my path? Show me what I need to work on and release.* There are times I am so tired and distraught that I simply say, *"God speak to me."* I look for the signs, words and feelings that come. God speaks to us in our creative thoughts, our inspiration, and God speaks to us through other people. They are the ones I refer to as, *Earth Angels* — the people who show up in my waking dreams to give me messages — often quite unbeknownst to them.

I write my questions and requests into my *Dream Journal* so that I may look at them again later to see exactly how they were written. It is very important when we wake from a dream, that we remember exactly how we worded the question. The wording of a question is vital to the answer we may receive. When you are new at working with your dreams, you may have difficulty understanding the information that you receive. Looking back to see how you worded the question will help you. Dreams are rarely literal, only prophetic dreams work in that way — and even they sometimes use symbols and metaphor to deliver their message. Our dreams are *symbolic* and we need to ask ourselves, *who or what is showing up now?* When you look at the people that show up in dreamtime, ask yourself, *how do I see them in waking life? What do they mean to me? What are their personalities like?* They could be family members, they could be friends, strangers, famous actors or actresses or people you know from childhood. You are the only interpreter of your world. You are the only one with the answers that come from within. Ask yourself, *what does this person represent in my waking life?* It may be that quality or characteristic that is important in your dream message, more so than the actual person.

There are many times when I reflect upon these personalities and figures for days. I have conversations with them, asking who they are and why they have shown up. The images are alive and are there to support you in this journey, to awaken you to new vision. Let your imagination run free and see what pops into your dreaming mind. It may surprise you! You may come to find a new world of dreamtime that opens doors to greater awareness, exciting exploration of creativity. Perhaps a darker aspect of dream may appear that is more frightening than exciting — remember, it is a dream to *awaken You. Keep Dreaming!*

More On How Dreams Speak

I have worked with many friends, family members and clients over the years. I love to see the progress and development in their own understanding of dreams. My wish is for them to learn how to be the Master of their own dream. We all have a slightly different "dictionary" with which to work, so the meaning of different symbols and images varies for each of us in relationship to the social and religious philosophies we have developed and into which we were born. For myself, I often wondered why my journey incorporated so many cultures, religions and philosophies; perhaps it was to better enable me to understand and help others. I am not limited to one understanding and expression. This has been a gift in my work with others.

I have a dear friend that I have been assisting in understanding dreams and the untapped possibilities they hold in opening our lives and careers in expansive ways. It has been about two years now and she has tapped into many possibilities. She knows there are no limits to what we can experience and explore in dreamtime. Her passion is her art and it is her career. She recently stepped out into the world and is sharing her gift of creativity in several galleries. She meditates devotedly, as another avenue to expand consciousness and shift her dreaming to another level.

One day she called me, very excited about what had just occurred:

She had just completed her meditation in which she was focusing on her art and prosperity. After her meditation, she fell back to sleep for a short nap. In her sleep, she felt herself traveling a distance to one of the galleries where her art is displayed. She was inside the gallery viewing or watching the gallery owner show her artwork. There was a person very interested in her art who asked the owner, "What process or technique does she use to acquire this look in her painting?"

She, my artist friend, realized the gallery owner could not explain the process to the woman questioning, as it was somewhat complicated. She also realized that this could cost her the sale of the painting. She had not sold a painting in that gallery yet as she was just featured in this gallery for two months. She knew she had to call the gallery owner and give him a better understanding to share with potential buyers.

She said that it felt like real life, "I was really there," she told me.

When she woke from this dream, she immediately contacted the gallery owner and told him she would email him a three-step process that he could share with anyone questioning her composition and technique. Two days later someone came into the gallery and asked about one of her paintings and, because of her recent email, he was able to share the technique with the client. *The painting was sold!* She was so excited about the sale and about the dream. She said to me, "I *finally get it! This stuff works!*"

It sure does! I was delighted and excited for her with the entire process. Her success continues and she is now living her dream.

The Words Are Here

Sometimes we receive messages in dreams in the form of actual words, rather than just visual images. Even words can be symbolic warnings, or direct messages. Many years ago I had the voice in my dream say, "Embody the dream." The power of the mind and the power of the words we speak hold a vibration that can heal and bring wholeness into our lives, unleashing the freedom and power of our Spirit. For me, to "embody the dream" means to fully feel and to truly work with the images and find their expression within me. It means to question, go deep and be curious about the nature of the dream. I have come to realize that my mind can manifest the dream and also the feeling — the embodiment can manifest into the physical. One example is this book. It was a thought, a dream, an embodied creation, that flowed onto the pages day by day. What I thought, dreamt, heard, saw, and embodied became manifest.

Here is an example of a dream I had in which the power of "the words" was expressed and shown to me ... Here is how the dream unfolded:

I was standing on an open green field; there was a man and woman waiting for someone. They needed to leave, but I knew they felt they couldn't leave without the arrival of these people. I offered to wait there and receive whomever they were expecting. I said to them, "I will wait and you can leave," so the couple left. Shortly after they had gone, a very large van pulled up carrying many horses. The horses were all sizes and colors; I heard over the loud speaker, "The words are here!"

I knew at that moment they had arrived. Of course, I thought the last name of the people I was waiting for was "Words." "The Words are here," (This is one example of a symbol in a dream which has a different meaning or is a 'play' on words.) Just then a very large — perhaps I should say a gigantic — *figure of a man standing eighteen feet in stature, got out of the horse van. I knew he was the person they had been expecting. He was wearing a necklace that resembled a very powerful amulet. He reminded me of a Shaman or Medicine Man. I felt the strength and intensity of the healing power this man held.*

I then woke up out of my sleep. I wrote the dream down before I lost it from my consciousness and reflected upon this dream. This is my practice in the morning before I go on to my meditation.

Here is what I understood about this dream. Horses have played a major part in many of my dreams over the years. This particular dream held a powerful message on several levels. First, I relate to horses as having great beauty, power, strength and freedom to roam the land. The horse was a gift from Spirit to the Indian, as it gave them great freedom to move about and enrich their lives. Because of my love of the Native American Indian and Benny's guidance, I have learned much about the Native ways, the animals, the land and the spiritual nature of things. My dreams reflect these things back to me. The man in my dream was of great stature. He represented a great symbol of *oneness with the earth and a sacred connection we have that needs to be honored and protected.* There was this large field in my vision or view, and now what showed up was this symbol of oneness and the power he carried with him — the horses. This power came in many sizes and many colors. I knew he held the gift of great wisdom in knowing about this power he carried. Now I had to learn about this powerful gift within myself. I knew that in order to understand this power I needed to become one with the nature of it. I knew I needed to spend more time with nature, learning the ways that nature speaks to us and the wisdom it holds. I remember the couple in the dream was waiting — *for the Words!* I knew the *Words held power!*

I must always remember the words I speak will leave a mark on any and all situations and people. I wish to stay conscious when presented with challenging situations. When we are aware of this we can respond in a way of wisdom and beauty. We can respond or pro-act in place of re-acting. There is a saying, "May I walk in beauty." What a great gift it would be to humanity if we could all remember those words and keep them in our hearts and minds. This earth would surely blossom.

This dream showed me the incredible tool we have through working with our dreams. Our soul speaks to us on so many levels. We have the gift of many opportunities for dreams to awaken us. We are moving in this *River of Dreams* called *Life*. Our story is coming alive, and we have an opportunity to listen and become a part of this story called *Self-Realization*. Our dreams are gifts to help us.

Within a year of having this dream, I started to do research, which included inquiring of others that were researching dreams on a more scientific level and on deeper levels of understanding the embodiment of dream. I had known and read about lucid dreaming research, but I wanted to deeply study *all* aspects of dream. I researched who was working on that level and who was continuing to expand and look deeper into the field that Carl Jung opened up to the world.

I continued to search and found a teacher-mentor with whom I could pursue a deeper study into dreaming. I was led to Pacifica Graduate Institute in Santa Barbara, California. There I found the mentor I was seeking, Dr. Steven Aizenstat. I inquired about his program, "Dreamtending," and found a possible avenue to delve deeper into the dreamtime. I filled out an application to attend and was accepted, however, due to my life situations at that time I did not join the classes. Time passed with my busy schedule and one night I had a dream. I heard the voice say, "*Call Pacifica today!*"

I remembered the classes and the challenge that would be possible as Dr. Aizenstat only accepted a small amount of students into each class. The classes were six-month sessions and I did not know when the next six months would start or whether I would have to apply again before I could be accepted into a class. I let go of the "mind talk" and listened to the words in the dream ..."Call Pacifica *today!*" It was a Friday morning and I made the phone call. I was told that a new class was starting at 6pm *that evening* and I could be there as they had someone cancel that morning! *That* was a sign!

I knew this was a wonderful opportunity, however, I had an appointment in L.A. on Saturday that would delay me until 1pm. I would not arrive in Santa Barbara until late afternoon on Saturday. I was told that it would be ok to arrive late, however, it was summertime and most likely I would not find a room in the Santa Barbara area at this late date. I replied, "Oh yes, I am sure I will as I know I am meant to come. I had a dream that told me to call *today!*"

I called every hotel and bed and breakfast that was listed in the directories. Everyone was booked, however two places told me if they had a cancellation they would call me. I knew the dream was directing me; my knowing came from experience and intuition. On Saturday morning I packed my bags, placed them in my car and headed off to L.A. and Santa Barbara. I had no doubt that I would get a call. Doubt can cancel out what we want to happen, so it is important to move forward with trust and faith. Saturday morning on a warm summer day, I began a journey that would lead to many wonderful friendships and experiences. Halfway up the 405 freeway to L.A., my cell phone ran and there it was, my room was ready for me. Someone had just canceled — just like the day before when someone canceled out of the class. I was in! What a magical, mystical experience. I believed, I trusted, and dreams can come true!

As I arrived at the entrance to "La Casa de Maria," and traveled the narrow private road that led to the loft, I came upon a thirteen-foot sculpture made of Carrara marble. It took my breath away and brought tears to my eyes. Here stood the beauty of the Native American and the Eagle. Together they were one and the inscription on this "Eagle Man," read: *Transformation through Forgiveness.* I was about to open another chapter in my life that would bring me into deep understanding of those words. I knew my dreams had led me in the right direction, there was no mistake in the feeling I held in my heart at that moment. I continued on the narrow road and reached the loft. "The Loft," was a large room that was overtop of a large garage on this land. I parked my car and stood facing the stairway that led to a room at the top. This is where I would come to know a deeper level of dreaming. I took a deep breath and climbed the stairway figuratively and literally. I stepped into a space where I would be learning a new way of relating to my dreams, as they began to speak to me in a new voice. My six-month study turned into five years of being in the landscape of dreamtime with a mentor — a wise elder of dreaming. I learned from his insight, his wisdom, his calm strength, and his understanding of holding the polarities of the opposites. You see, we must embrace the shadow in order to do our healing work. The dreams we call nightmares must be embraced and faced. It is like looking fear right in the eye. He showed us how to use these dream figures as our allies. He taught from that inner understanding and compassion. Most of all I learned from his silence. Silence is truly a gift of a wise teacher. As I look back and review the five years I spent expanding my visions and dreams, I realize that through this process I opened to a deep level of forgiveness for myself and for others. Just as the statue had foretold five years earlier: "Transformation Through Forgiveness." Those years were years of tears, pain and joy. I know that my dream had led me there for healing on many levels, and the dream was an answer to many questions. Again I recognized that our answers come over time and with patience. During these years, I found friendship and compassion, laughter and tears, while embracing all that was and is today. I was guided to join those of like mind and heart and in the willingness to jump into the unknown. I was given incredible friends I call "sisters." Steve, as I refer to Dr. Aizenstat today, was a gift out of dreamtime.

The Awake Dream

I have come to realize that I am always dreaming, even when I am awake. The "waking dream" is at work when we realize that everything we experience in a waking state holds meaning and messages for us, just as they do in a dream state. Life is a rich field of metaphor and meaning — if we take the time to pay attention and notice the signs all around us. Again, journaling our daily experiences — especially the ones that are out of the ordinary — is really helpful for making sense of them. You see, I never want to miss an opportunity to change the script, especially if it can be written better. So, here again is one of my waking dreams that also relates to the horses that appear night and day.

Just recently I traveled to Cambria, California, on a little retreat. It was very difficult to receive cell phone communication in most of that area, so I would need to go down the hillside to have a connection and make a phone call. One day I drove down to a spot where I could use my phone to retrieve my messages and return phone calls. I pulled over to the side of the road and proceeded to make a call to a friend of mine. The conversation had gone in a direction that had to do with how to stand in my own power. I had probably been on the phone for 30 minutes or so; I was about to hang up, when I felt as if someone was staring at me. As I turned my head to the right there was a very large

horse with a beautiful blonde mane staring right into my car window!
Two blondes starring at one another. A little bit of a shock, I must say.
You see, I had parked the car right up against a fence that was a pasture.
I had not even noticed when I stopped the car, or perhaps there were
no horses in view at that time. Talk about waking symbols! Yes, horses
have followed me *day and night*! Power and freedom has always been by
my side and now it was starring me in the face; I almost ignored it. I'm
learning to ride that power gently with respect and the right use of it.

There Are Messages And Messengers

As I have mentioned previously, I always ask for guidance and
request that I recognize when I am being given a message, as the
messenger can show up in many forms. What I have worked towards
is finding a knowing within myself when there is an *Ah Ha!* — a gut
feeling that someone or something is trying to show up with a powerful
message for me. I am always watching and testing the waters to see if
the metaphor is "in my face" as the saying goes, and to recognize when
I may be in denial about what an experience is trying to tell me. When
we keep open to the messengers and try to have some fun with this
practice, we begin to see the message — and our denial — easier and
faster. Here is an example of a *"waking dream" in which the messenger
could have easily been denied, and the message missed entirely.*

During the time I was traveling back and forth from the east
coast to the west coast I had purchased a toll pass called *"The Fast
Trak."* The pass is placed onto your windshield, therefore when you
are traveling on a toll road you do not need to stop at the tollbooth.
This item registers the information on your car and your credit card
is automatically charged with the amount when you pass through the
toll gate. I drove on this highway many times and there was never

a problem. On this particular day my girlfriend and I were driving along anticipating a great day of fun and shopping. We were on the toll road when I looked into my rear view mirror and saw lights flashing from a patrol car. I could not imagine that they were flashing for me; I am very careful about speed and I have a monitor on my car that alerts me when I am going over the speed limit. I knew I was fine and my registration was up-to-date, so what could possibly be the problem? My girlfriend became concerned and we pulled over. The officer and I had the following conversation.

"I need to see your license and registration."

"What is the problem officer?"

"Do you realize that your are driving on this toll road with a Fast Trak?"

"Yes, I do. What is the problem with that?"

"You have a Florida license plate and a Fast Trak. You can not have a Fast Trak unless you live in California."

"I have two homes, one in Florida and one in California."

"Do you go back and forth?"

"Yes, I do."

"You cannot have a Fast Trak with an out of state license plate. I think you better decide which state you want to drive your car in."

"Officer, are you saying I can not have two homes and drive this car in both places? I don't understand, since they gave me the Fast Trak knowing my car is registered in Florida."

"You need to decide which state you wish to reside in."

"Are you telling me I have to leave this state if I want to keep this license plate?"

"I am not telling you to leave, just make a choice! I will not give you a ticket, but you decide. The car that you drive here in California must be registered in this state!"

"Thank you officer, I will give this consideration."

Now, as we drove away, my girlfriend was very upset that he had told me I could only drive the car in one state and didn't believe that I couldn't have a Fast Trak on my car with an out of state plate, as long as I was paying the tolls. I had a smile on my face and she did not quite understand that I was not the least bit upset. You see, as the officer and I were having the conversation, I immediately went into *"message-messenger"* thinking. This was a "waking dream" message! The officer was the messenger from a higher power and stopped me in order to help me understand where I stood in the rules and responsibility of the way I was driving *through my life*. The car I drive is my way of moving through life and getting where I needed to go. The way I was moving was caught between *two states*. I saw that as a metaphor: *two states of consciousness!* One state of consciousness was still registered on the east coast, where I had come from. I was now moving in a *different state of consciousness on the west coast*. I was being warned that I could not drive in a responsible way in *both states!* I realized that even though I had moved from one state, I was still registering in the other state of consciousness. Wow, isn't that an awakening?! It sure was for me. He was a kind and generous messenger and did not ticket me. It did not cost me anything for this delay of transfer, however, if I did not make the decision soon, it would certainly cost me down the road.

I could have been frustrated, and angry, and experienced several other emotional upsets over getting pulled over; however, this was *a big message from a higher power!*

This is a great tool to use when we need to look at the way we perceive a situation. Moments such as these are crossroads where we have the option whether to become powerful or become the victim of circumstance.

I knew that I was holding onto something from the past. I needed to ask myself what it was that kept me moving within two states. What was my fear in letting go of the past? This was a crossroad where fear and power met and I choose to move into a clear, aware State of Consciousness. I am now registered in that *state*! It is a good feeling when we let go and trust. My friend was shocked at what had just happened and, as I shared this awareness with her, she began to have the same big smile on her face that I did, as she, too, became aware of the power of the metaphor. We both continued on and had the most exciting day you can imagine!

A "waking dream" can either be something very simple, or a large *Ah Ha*; it doesn't matter. Start dreaming — *dreaming awake* in the daylight hours and see how interesting it can be. Recording your experiences in a journal will help you to make sense of them, and to recognize the metaphor and the messengers when they arrive in your life. Sometimes, when something is happening, you get caught up in the emotions of the moment — like when you get pulled over by a police officer — and it isn't until afterwards when you are journaling that you realize the message.

Questions to meditate upon:

Where are the messengers and messages in my daily life?

What are the metaphors showing me? Think of one experience that happened in the past week or two. Meditate upon a deeper meaning than you had experienced.

Ask yourself:

Can I give myself the permission to take pen to paper and just let the feelings speak?

Your journal is a place where there is no judgment. Let go of the critic. Feel and express what is inside. This is another tool to transmute the pain, grief, sadness and fear into something powerful.

Notes

_____

_____

_____

_____

_____

_____

_____

_____

_____

_____

_____

_____

_____

_____

_____

_____

_____

_____

_____

_____

_____

_____

_____

_____

_____

_____

_____

_____

_____

_____

Chapter Seven: Tracking the Dreams

"Dreams can chart and further the healing process for mind, body and spirit."

—Carl Jung.

Dreams are primarily symbolic, and most of the time we are all of the characters in the dream, or the essence of the characters. The objects can pertain to things that are in our lives or happening in our lives — the struggles, defeats, successes, wins and losses. The things that have happened in our activities of the day, and the things we continually think of consciously and subconsciously. Dreams continue to be reflections of our thoughts. Dreams mirror back to us what we need to look at. If you are dreaming — and remembering what you are dreaming — then you are ready to look at it. These issues are coming up to shine light upon them and you are ready for work, my friends. It's like a big detective story and you are ready to find the clues to what is happening — in *your life*! With some courage and faith, dig deep into your pillows at night and know that your soul is calling you to awaken.

Keeping Track

Tracking dreams is a vital tool in understanding where we have been and where we are headed. There are times when I am given a second dream that adds more information to the previous dream. When we don't track our dreams, it is easy to think each dream is isolated and only relevant to that moment in time, but by tracking them over time, we start to see how they are weaving a story throughout our lives, and how the dreams connect to each other. This may also be a way we begin to connect to the collective. When we keep track of and share dreams with our friends, we may begin to realize we are not dreaming alone. I have found that truth for myself while working within dream groups. When you work closely with a dream group on a weekly or monthly basis, you begin to dream collectively. The story line is shared between one or two others in the group. There have been times when the entire group had the same theme in their dream. This is another example that we are connected, and more proof in understanding the power of the mind and thoughts. First we have thoughts, then thoughts become the dream, and then the dream becomes our reality. With this experience and realization I have become very conscious of my thoughts — what I read, look at or meditate upon — before I go to sleep in the evening.

When you begin a dream journal, leave room at the front or back for an index or Table of Contents. Be sure to date each dream as you record them and add the date to the index. Give each dream a title, like a chapter in a book. For example: "Oct. 3, 2006, Butterfly Woman Speaks." Then add a page number so you can easily find the dream later. If there is an overriding theme or quality to your dream, make a note of it in the index. For example, "Panther dream" or "Flying dream" or "Healing dream." Indexing your dreams will make easy to look up the themes running through your RIVER OF DREAMS at different times in your life. We will then have a way to recognize the phases and progress we are making. By keeping a more detailed record of our other realities (dreams), we will become more *aware* of our actions and the consequences — cause and effect — also known as *karma*. By doing this, we will begin to see a familiar pattern to our dreams, our story. This index will save time and help you to see where you have traveled and the progress in the evolution of your soul. With *Tracking,* we begin to connect the dots, since the theme can take place over a period of time but not necessarily in an obvious continuum. If you follow this suggested format, you will become more *aware* of your journey. This is a way of creating a Road Map of Dreams.

For example, I was asked by one of my mentors to go back into my journals and find all the dreams that connected me to the Native American Indians. She wanted me to look back and understand the level of influence the dream patterns had on my spiritual journey connected to the Native American Culture. She wanted me to reflect upon how the two worlds come together in this physical reality. What messages had I realized? Where were the connections in my life today?

Over the years of experiencing and journaling visions and dreams, I developed this awareness of tracking. Earlier in my journaling dreams, I was just happy to wake up, get the dreams down into my journal, and get back to sleep. So, I do understand the patience and determination it takes to be faithful to this practice. In order to answer this woman's question, I had to go back into two large boxes of dream journals and find the dreams that took me into the world of the indigenous people. As I reviewed them, I began to realize the years of dreamtime that connected the threads and were weaving my story.

One of the first connecting threads I found was a young black haired Indian maiden, dressed in white buckskin. She visited in dreamtime over several years. She appeared the first time with the breeze moving through her long silky black hair as I watched her walk forward away from my view. She would show up about once every several months for two years. I never saw her face as she was always walking away from me. Now that I look back, perhaps she was leading me and guiding me on a path, on a Spirit Walk. She may have been connecting me to nature and the way of the medicine women.

These dreams started back in the early eighties. During those months and years that she appeared, I also had the dreams that spoke to me of other Native American Indian ceremonial symbols. She stopped visiting my dreams in the mid-nineties. I had forgotten all about her until one day in February, 2006. This visit in February was very important, as she (the Indian Maiden) was asked to take a stand in the sacred waters of life. She was not given a choice; she was told *she would stand in these waters until she did!* Once I had stepped on to this path and realized my prayers were to be awakened to a greater understanding and to be of service unto myself and others, the choices changed. It wasn't just any choice. My choices had to come from deep meditation from within, my motivation and intentions had to come from the heart with clear perceiving. I had to remember to walk in the beauty way.

As I continued to search my journals, I came to realize who she was and how her journey was carefully and divinely being guided. I realized I had much to learn from the ancestors and great understanding to embrace in order to live in compassion and integrity. The River of Dreams calls us all to move in the flow of life's waters and *remember who we are.*

I spent days upon days searching for this information. There were connections I had forgotten about. Thank God for the journals I kept. I never would have remembered all these dreams, let alone the details, if I hadn't written it all down. I have now come to understand the *gift of dream* on another level. When the dreams were recorded, I had no idea where they were taking me. There are times when we just need to dream and make the change before we can understand why it was necessary. I had great *trust* and *faith*, which is most important. I now recognize how Great Spirit was moving me in the direction of *inner truth. I had to surrender!* The journals have been a precious and valuable tool for me for sharing my story. The unfolding takes time and patience.

When we track our dreams, they become the example of how our lives are inter-woven and interconnected to our spiritual and physical world. The tracking has been proof to me that the two worlds are not separate. They are truly one and the same; the pieces come together. If we have the tools and directions to put the pieces together, then we can go back and realize; we can begin to remember. I now have given all the dreams with the Indian Maiden the title "She Who Remembers." I realize now that the River of Dreams *does flow by itself*—we do not need to push it. We do need to ask for help in *remembering*. Once again, I remind you that you must ask the question; then you have the possibility of receiving an answer. May I say, a strong possibility.

The natural ways of the Native American felt true to me, and perhaps the dreams that continue to come and go as the years pass continue to align and awaken that closeness to nature that I found as a small child. The animals, the land, the flowers and the streams that I played in, were and are natural to me. This has been a continuous river flowing through my dreams, a recurring theme throughout my life.

The following experience is an example of how, at times, I only receive a *verbal dream (or the voice that speaks)*, no pictures; the screen is blank and I only receive *whispers in the dark*.

BLACK ELK SPEAKS

In the middle of the night I heard whispers, the voice was very clear. One night I heard, *Black Elk Speaks! Black Elk Speaks!* I awoke and looked around the room. Of course, I was stunned to find no one there, or perhaps I was *relieved* to find no one there!!! Wow, I knew that since the voice was so clear, this was important and I had to write it down *immediately*. I doubted if I could ever forget something so clear and profound as that, but you never know. I followed my own instructions and wrote everything down.

I thought about this the next day and contemplated the book about *Black Elk* that I had read many years prior to having this dream experience. I had a gut feeling or intuition that this was something I needed to be patient with and time would unfold the truth of what was to be revealed. I had to be very patient. In fact, it was so long in the unfolding that I had actually forgotten about the voice in the dream. Several years passed.

One day I was on a journey through Sedona; I stopped at an art gallery that contained many art pieces and jewelry, reflective of the Native American Indian. As I glanced into one of the jewelry cases I was shocked to see a necklace with three symbols that had shown up in a dream six months prior. I had asked for a dream that would show me the symbols for the healing energy work I was pursuing, and information to create a logo for my business card. Well, there was the necklace with my three symbols. Wasn't that amazing that Spirit actually created my symbols in a necklace for me! The three symbols were a staff, a hand, and a circle, and placed upon the staff was a beautiful back raven. I immediately expressed my surprise and excitement by saying, "*That was made for me!*"

The women behind the counter replied, "It absolutely belongs to you."

She took it out of the case and as I reached for it she said these exact words, "*Black Elk Speaks.*"

I gasped for breath and started to cry. The poor woman was stunned and came around the counter to help me compose myself. She said she was so sorry, she did not mean to say that. What she *wanted* to say was that Wallace Black Elk was coming from North Dakota to the Unity Church in Sedona that night and she wanted to invite me to attend with her. She had felt that it was important for me to see him.

Once I caught my breath and composed myself, I shared that she was perfectly correct in speaking those *exact words* as that was the message I was to receive. I shared the dream with her that came several years earlier and unfolded as she spoke. I also shared the experience I had in regard to the necklace and the dream that presented those exact symbols. She was, of course, amazed, and I, needless to say, accepted the invitation to join her and Black Elk.

The evening was filled with gratitude, excitement and tears. Snow was falling lightly and the red mountains sparkled with a golden orange-pink evening glow. For Black Elk, the road he had to travel was not an easy journey. I sat in awe, in anticipation, waiting to hear his footsteps enter the church. Blazing chills rushed through my veins as he stepped up onto the platform, opened his arms and welcomed us. There were only twenty of us in that church that evening. I could not believe that the church was not bursting at the seams with people; however, those of us that needed to be there were.

Black Elk spoke these words to us, "Those of you that have come tonight, do not question any longer your heritage, for those of you that sit here tonight are our ancestors returned in the white man." My prayers had been answered from my childhood. I had long given up the search. I had surrendered, meaning I no longer was attached to the outcome. I no longer had the deep searching desire. I came to a place of peace within. I told Spirit that I would not question my ancestry any longer. I trusted Spirit to give me the answer when and if I was to know where my tree was rooted, *Spirit Answered!*

More tears; my newly acquired friend was about to rename me, "She-who-Cries-a-lot." There is still more, just wait — patience is a virtue!

Black Elk shared how difficult it was for him to step forward into a church after all that had happened to his people in the name of God. I believe he said that it was the first time for him to be in this place. I felt his pain and his incredible strength and wisdom. This was a man who, in my understanding, came from a place of "Transformation through forgiveness." Here lies the place of deep understanding. I now reflect back to the statue of Eagle Man at Casa de Maria. Black Elk and his people had suffered so many wounds, yet here he was sharing his stories so that others might learn.

We all have stories to tell within our own families, communities, our countries and the world. We are all brothers and sisters. Our stories must be told. They must be shared so we can remember how to walk in beauty together on this earth — with respect for all people. We must have loving kindness even as we each travel a different road and hear a different drum. We all are longing for peace within

What a gift I had received that evening. His knowledge and wisdom touched my heart. He shared that his education was very limited in the public school system. He had not been educated in the higher grades, and yet had the knowledge and wisdom of a professor. This was truly an evening of great joy. As I continued to drink in the wine of his words, I listened with my heart to what came next. He said he wanted to explain to us a ceremony that is performed to call in the ancestors

He told us the first thing they would do is gather a long staff and take a Raven and bind it to the top of the staff, and once it was bound safely, never harmed, they prayed and called to the ancestors. When the ancestors answered their calling, they would then set the raven free to take flight. I sat there with chills running through my spine as I touched my hand to my new necklace. There upon my neck lay raven, "*With wings to fly!*"

My dreams were becoming my reality. My dreams and my waking life flow with no separation, except for the separation that my mind creates. If we can change our dreams, we can change our reality. What are our dreams showing us? How can we learn from the messages? We can dream a different dream. I realized through these experiences that I can live a *different reality*.

I recall another dream while traveling towards the "Four Corners," land of the Native American Indians. I had stopped to rest overnight, as the journey was long. That is when I had this dream. I was in Flagstaff, Arizona.

DREAM:

I was on a road and walking along; I heard a thunderous noise. I realized, within seconds, that there were herds and herds of Buffalo coming towards me. Actually, they were everywhere. It was like a stampede, but I was not injured nor even harmed in any way. I was actually observing, perhaps even in the middle of it all, but unaware that they were coming.

I awoke with a feeling of amazement and questioned what I was not aware of that was coming to me in all directions. Knowing that this dream was a profound message from Spirit, I wrote it down and thought I would look at it along the way ... and I did just that. What

I have come to recognize is that it is a symbol for abundance as well as the ability to manifest this through right action and prayer, and to honor what has been given to me. I realized the message was a reminder to seek the Divine in all that I do. If I follow the understanding of the buffalo and honor the Spiritual Journey I am on, then I shall be given all that I need. You see, I must realize the difference between all that I *need* and all that I *want*.

The Buffalo was a very sacred animal to the Native American and I was on the path to the native lands, literally and figuratively. I was surrounded by abundance. As the years have passed I now look back and see the symbols that were opening me to a new world of beauty and a new way to "*walk in beauty.*"

When I arrived to the land of the Dine' Indians, I was greeted once more by my friend Jerald. He was ready to take me on new land that he had not shown to me before. As we entered this land he told me he would walk in front of me calling prayers to the ancestors. I followed. He walked several feet ahead of me chanting, *"May you walk in beauty." This was a time of many, many blessings that are still unfolding.*

I say to you, my precious reader, "May you dream your dream, weave your tapestry, and may you walk in beauty."

Never doubt the Gift of Dream and the promise of Spirit, for I have experienced the greatness of knowing the answers will come, surrendering to a greater power than I could ever begin to imagine.

My dreams are intertwined with other cultures and other passions, but the American Indian thread is strong. I believe we must follow the threads that weave *Our Story.* Listen and watch to pick-up the *yarn* that will carry you to a place where you will recognize the beginning of your tapestry. Imagine the colorful coat that you may wear for warmth, tenderness, comfort and strength. Like Joseph, in the Bible, who had the beautiful coat of many colors.

Questions to meditate upon and a visualization exercise:

What would it take to "spread your wings?"

How would it be to move forward into unknown territory? Now, Imagine going where you have never gone before, with courage and trust. Relax, close your eyes and visualize this journey. An Indian guide has come to you. You can see him or her clearly as your hand is taken gently into their hand; you move down a beautiful pathway that leads into a garden. In the garden is a rainbow bridge; you are willing to take this step with courage to walk hand in hand over this bridge to the unknown. There is a gift waiting for you when you return. As you walk over the bridge, remember you are not ever alone. Let yourself take flight into a new experience. After you have this new experience you walk back over the bridge and there is a gift waiting for you back in the garden where you began. Accept the gift that is yours.

Trust, patience, courage, prayer and dreaming will awaken new vistas for you to spread your wings and fly.

Notes

_____

_____

_____

_____

_____

_____

_____

_____

_____

_____

_____

_____

_____

_____

_____

_____

_____

_____

_____

_____

_____

_____

_____

_____

_____

_____

_____

Chapter Eight:
The Healer Within

"That which does not kill us makes us stronger."

— *Nietzsche*

Dream Practice offers a holistic healing and spiritual approach; I have personally experienced the healing results from practicing dream questing. This is truly a very powerful tool for healing our own minds and bodies, on various levels.

In the summer of 2002, my world was struck with a thunderbolt. A crises came into my life that could have either destroyed my belief in everything I knew, or else it could have become a cracking open, a perception of a new and stronger ground to stand upon for the rest of my life. This was the day that I was told my daughter had A.L.S. As I mentioned in my introduction, I have been asked many times, *"How do you live in peace and joy when your world crashes in front of your eyes?* "The material in this book contains all of the preparatory work, as well as the foundation that allowed me to move forward with courage and strength, to be able to hold the space for a miracle to take place.

They say, "When one door closes another opens." I have found that to be very true throughout my life. I have come to recognize the courage it takes to allow the doors to gently close, although there are times they just slam in your face. With conscious decision-making we can walk with gentle steps on this path. Through our mistakes and the willingness to perceive greater understanding of ourselves and others, we can hold the space for love to create and build new foundations for healthier lives. My decision to journey out on my own as a single woman, and follow Spirit and my passions, challenged me to open a closed door, to move in and through the darkness and pain, in order to build understanding and strength. Many times I had only my faith to bring me into another day. It took courage to take one more breath that would lead me to choose another way of seeing what had been hidden from view. These were the times that I picked myself up over and over and knew there was a power greater than I that brought me into new understanding and greater inner wisdom. Those years were *the foundation—the rock* that I stood strong upon when the question was presented to me, "How can you be at peace when you have a daughter diagnosed with a life-threatening illness?"

There are times that we have no idea why we are traveling down a road and we take the fork to the right or to the left. We trust, we pray, we dream our way in the *River* and flow with the current. If we have to swim against the current, it's a struggle, but there are times we must do that also. We never know where the river will take us and upon what shore we will walk. When we need to rest we need to go to the riverbank and get out; that's just the way it is. Other times we have no choice and we just keep paddling.

After my daughter's diagnosis there were many times I could not meditate or find a place to be still within. Tears flowed and my heart broke, but I knew that there was a place to surrender and give it to a greater power. My journey had given me that "gift."

One day I had a dream that told me I had to play music. I continued to have the dream over and over. Listening to music has always been a healing, relaxing and joyous activity in my life. I could not understand why the dream continued, as I never had the innate ability to be a musician. One day when I was visiting my daughter and my two grandchildren in Alabama, I found my four-year-old grandson with a guitar. He said, "I really want to learn to play my guitar." That was all I needed to hear — off we went to guitar lessons. I watched his very small fingers desperately trying to reach each string to bring the sound of joy to our ears. I realized then that I had the *same wish!* The teacher told me he had a good friend who owned a guitar shop near my home in California. Upon my return home I dashed out to buy my guitar and find my teacher.

When I told the owner of the shop that I wanted to play the guitar because I could feel the notes and vibrations run from my heart down to my fingers, he said, *"I have the one and only teacher for you!"*

Yes, indeed he did! I started immediately and not a day too soon, as far as I was concerned. This was joy to my heart; the strings called the music of Spirit to me. As I was playing, the pain of my daughter's situation would crash through my thoughts and crack my heart open. The music soothed my wounds and helped me to connect with the deep place within me where previously mediation would take me. Music provided a new route to my heart and served as another great tool for healing. Music and the guitar touched me deep within, as if I were strumming my heartstrings. My teacher referred to that often; he would tell me that the guitar was an instrument that allowed me to feel deeply as my fingers plucked each string. The dream to "play music" wasn't guidance to play music on a CD, but to literally play music as the musician. The dreams "prescription" was the best "therapy" possible for helping me process my emotions over my daughter.

Days carried into weeks and on to months. Sometimes challenges become gifts and gifts become challenges. Playing music was a new meditation for me and it allowed me to resume my other meditations; what a blessing! Well, like my little grandson, I also had small hands and tiny fingers. I struggled and struggled, but the pain in my wrist invaded my pleasure. The pain continued into my forearm, but I continued to fight in order to play. Inflammation developed in my tendons. I tried months of alternative medical treatments. Finally, I made an appointment with an Orthopedic Doctor who had operated on my right wrist ten years prior. That surgery was necessary due to severe inflammation in the tendons. I had tried many alternative treatments back than, but finally had to have surgery to release the sheaves on the tendons for them to heal. This time it was my left wrist and I had to stop playing the guitar. Again, the doctor suggested surgery, but I wanted to continue to look for an alternative to surgery. He told me that he understood, however, I did not need to return unless I wanted to go ahead with the surgery.

He said, " If I don't see you again, I will know you healed your wrist. If not, I will meet you in the O.R.!"

I continued and it only got worse, so I gave in and scheduled the date to meet him in the Operating Room on July 26th. On July 23rd I had the following dream:

In this dream a voice said, "Cancel surgery." Then there was a sign placed in front of my eyes that said, "Detoxify your body!"

Wow, I usually ask for another dream to confirm what my dreams are saying, but I did not *Question* this one. I knew I was being guided from the "*Healer within.*" I knew I had no time to waste. I immediately cancelled the surgery! I then proceeded to contact my family physician and made an appointment to see her. I told her about my dream, as she knew this was a major part of the way I lived my life and that I listened to messages and messengers. She immediately told me she knew what treatment she was to prescribe — a detoxification program that is done with a light beam generator, and then you are placed in an infrared sauna. There are also herbs given to help detoxify the body during this process. The treatment was done in three sessions, which took place two weeks apart.

After my first session I began to feel very tired and beads of moisture oozed from my skin with small rough pimple like protrusions appearing on my face and neck. This was the process of toxins being eliminated, but the pain persisted. I could feel something different inside my arm and wrist, as if cells were shifting. After the second session I had the same symptoms, however, this time the pain started to release from the forearm. The only pain left was in the wrist and thumb. In the third session I had extreme exhaustion, which I was told was natural. Detoxifying is a challenge; I may have been exhausted, but my cells were more than likely dancing for joy. They must have been saying, "I'm alive again, I'm alive again!"

Then the pain started to release from my wrist and thumb. I now could turn my hand over without a struggle. The pain continued to release and I fully recovered —without surgery. I longed to return to the guitar, however, I remain today just listening to the *"strings of my heart."* This was a profound teaching on many levels. First, to live our passion, play the music and listen to the heartstrings! Take the chance of returning to the child within. We can listen to the music and release pain that is held deep within our cells. Secondly, to pay attention to the wisdom of our bodies, that is often revealed in dreams. There are so many "signposts" here in this story. When we listen to the *Healer within, we* know we have a choice to choose another way.

There were many gifts that came from this experience, and doors that opened while I was writing this chapter. While my daughter continues to manage the health challenges placed in her life, there have been a series of miracles both large and small that have given us all hope that she will be able to regain her strength and beat this challenge. While this is an entirely different story filled with lessons and miracles, dreams and, yes, disappointments, as well as a hopeful re-diagnosis. I will leave them for her to write about when she is well. Let it suffice for now to say that I continue to hold her in my prayers, in my meditations and in my heart, while I watch my dreams for the divine guidance to reveal to me anything I may need to see. While this is happening to *her* physical body, this illness is affecting the *emotional* body of everyone who loves her and cares for her. Thus, it is important to stay aware of what may be revealed, as powerful lessons to each of us. Dreams and journaling can bring forth the inner healer of both body and spirit.

Alchemy to Healing

When we receive messages about illness we need to ask if this is a *real* problem that exists, a potential that one will show up, or whether the illness is symbolic of something else we need to look at. Always address the fact that we may be receiving either a warning or help that can lead to prevention. Once we intuitively know we are fine, or we have a clean bill of health, then we can address it as symbolic. The psyche has a way of speaking to us in symbols; the mind has a very unique nature and we need a new dictionary to understand its messages. As you pay attention and track your dreams, you will start to see the way your spirit, your intuition, speaks to you. You will begin to learn the language and will create your own dictionary along the way; it's an interesting and fun process. You will be finding out about yourself in a very unique way.

It is the same when my car shows up in a dream and I am told there is a problem, or I have a flat tire, engine problems, etc. Again, I make sure my car in running in tip top shape, so I check out the logical — the literal. If the literal realm is in order, I move to the symbolic. Sometimes the "logical" is about how I am moving through life, and it's all symbolic. If so, it is time to head back to the drawing board to weave the threads together. Intuitively, we generally know if the dream is symbolic or literal, but we should never just ignore the potential for a warning given in a dream. When a messenger shows up, heed the warning! This is true for both sleeping and awake dreams!

We must remember that most dreams are symbolic. With practice, you will get used to the flow and recognize the symbols and the feelings held within your dream. If you remember the guidelines along the way that I have given you, it won't take long.

Imaginary time .... imaginary space .... that is where dreams are made. Can you *imagine* that? Well, there are many who have, like Edison. He saw the light before he invented it. Many great inventions and problems have been solved in that space of time or no time, called dreaming.

Dream Healing

The study and practice of dreams for healing purposes goes back to the Ancient Greeks and Egyptians. Mythology speaks of the Greek healing God *Asclepius,* who was the patron of physicians, a true healer through a path of deeper discovery. He worked many healings through dreams and visions. He can appear in a dream in many guises: God, bearded man, boy, snake, or dog. There are many pilgrims that travel to Epidauros, which is on the eastern Peloponnesian coast near the

Saronic Gulf. They go in search of the mystery that is revealed in the healings and teachings of Asclepius.

I realized, at the request of a friend, that I would take my research a step further and surrender to the unknown. I would journey to the sacred healing sites at Athens, Korinth, Krete, and the most famous site of Epidauros. I traveled with a group led by Dr. Edward Tick, the author of "The Practice of Dream Healing." This journey was offered to me very unexpectedly and I agreed to journey into the land of Ancient Greek Mysteries and find the door that would open into "the healer within." I had read Dr. Tick's book four years prior to this journey. This was a book that gripped me tight as I held onto every experience and teaching found within its intriguing pages. I was overjoyed and surprised to hear of this opportunity to travel and experience first hand what Dr. Tick knew and experienced at a deep personal level. I knew *destiny* was knocking at my door. This was again one of those signposts I refer to. I needed to walk through that doorway to experience the embodied dream — to live the dream. I was open to whatever waited on the other side. Well, not quite … there was *some* hesitation. Complications arose with airline scheduling and my dearest friend, who was going to travel with me, cancelled! I had to do it alone! Not that I haven't adventured over many seas and mountains alone before, but I was looking forward to her arrival in Athens to celebrate the auspicious occasion of my birthday. I refer to this as auspicious due to the dreams that were showing me there was a rebirth at my doorway. Perhaps on every birthday it is a rebirth! It certainly seemed auspicious to me, as this one would occur in Greece, where dream healing began. When I heard about my friend's cancellation I immediately contacted Dr. Tick and shared with him my doubts. His reply was "Hermes is trying to see if you truly want to make this journey." That was all he had to say, as just weeks prior to all of the news to travel to Greece I had a dream visitation from Hermes, yes, winged hat and all. You see, when he visited me, he said nothing. He just appeared and was gone in seconds, but I knew he had a message of some kind and I had to wait for it to appear in a sign. I knew he would show up again in some form. This was it! Dr. Tick was the messenger for Hermes. This was another signpost. Hermes was testing me, *or was he tripping me up?* Hermes is the Greek God of travel and he is also known as the trickster. They (Hermes *and* Ed Tick) got me. I knew I was being challenged by the Gods before I even left California.

I arrived in Athens Greece on February 17, 2006, my birthday. The Gods and Goddesses were awaiting. Talk about timing — sometimes it's *everything*! Of course, when you agree to go on pilgrimage, the journey starts the moment you agree. I had several dreams that preceded my arrival in Greece. There were many events that took place years prior to this journey that revealed themselves as I took the steps onto the land of Ancient Mysteries. Trust and faith once again revealed more clarity about dreams that I had experienced five years earlier. I began to place the pieces of the puzzle together from my night-voyages of dreams into the experiences that were occurring each day of the journey. I began to realize the process of purification that was described in dream temples of Asclepius. It was the first process in preparation before asking for a dream of healing. I realized I had been preparing all along. In the time of Asclepius, they would first take the sacred baths.

There are times that we clear out old ways of thinking, unhealthy habits, and relationships that no longer server us, in order to prepare us for the work ahead. I viewed this as a purification process (the sacred bath). This is how I saw my process in action, although the ancient ritual way to prepare for the ancient dream incubation was the literal mineral springs and baths. That is something we can still do. It is truly a beautiful ritual and sets the tone and intention. I often prepare the bath with mineral salts, light a candle and sometime add the music of the angelic realms. I often view the process in many new ways, keeping in mind my spiritual practice. Meditation is a regular preparatory practice that I do before entering the nighttime dream process. The journey in Greece held continual rituals during which we were called to re-establish our strengths and to show up to support each other in seeing the truth of compassion. We came to understand the inter-connectedness, and realizing that support from each one held the vibration for healing. We each had dreams of our own as well as dreams for each other. The stage was set and the drama was in the dream, both awake and asleep. It is not unlike the plays of ancient times on the stages of Greek Myth. The orators of days gone by echoed in our thoughts and minds and played on the stage of our dreams.

Many of my past dreams of Egyptian Gods and Goddesses wove their presence with the Greek Gods and Goddesses to reveal once again, that there is no separation. We are all one and inter-related in our body/mind intentions. We all have our struggles, desires, hopes and dreams. A journey such as this one is truly embodying the dream and was a dream come true for "The Dreamer." We lived the dream; we were the actors and players of the drama we created day and night. We would clear the stage and continue the next act, perhaps on another stage on another Greek Isle, but we never left our fellow players and dreamers behind.

Asclepius walked on this earth in ancient times and ushered in the foundation of dreams as a healing process. Some say he was the first psychiatrist; perhaps so. Whatever he stood for or came to do, he is remembered by Greece in sanctuaries throughout the islands. The Greeks looked to many of the Gods and Goddesses for their healing abilities. Isis has been connected to the temples of dreaming in Egypt. She was the Goddess of Dreaming. She appeared to me in dreamtime several years ago before this journey to Greece. On this pilgrimage at Epidaurus, I was reunited with the connection she had with Asclepius. Upon the grounds where the Asclepion temple is now being resurrected at Epidaurus is also a temple under construction for Isis. What a shock it was to find her there at Epidaurus. I traveled across the oceans to find the God and Goddess of Dream Healing! I had the following dream about Isis five years prior to my journey to Greece.

THE DREAM UNFOLDS:

I saw a black panther. He came towards me and I slowly melded into his being and moved about as panther. I, as Panther, moved towards a wooden horse. This horse resembled the wooden horse of Helen of Troy. I was then inside the horse, and as it moved I sensed that we were entering a mysterious place. Yes, it was a pyramid. We entered and were taken down into a deep chamber below the earth. Then a door opened and the wooden horse moved forward out of the first chamber into another chamber. I, Panther, was still inside. Just then, a door opened in the horse and I moved forward. I was now peering out of the brilliant green eyes of Anubis. Panther had shifted into Anubis. I looked up and seated on a throne in front of me was the Goddess Isis!

The dream ended and I awakened.

There is much written about Isis and the Temple of Dreaming. This was no accident that she came to me in the way she did, and allowed the dream to play out in my waking dream on the Greek Islands. Once again patience and time reveals the dream. I understand the dream in this way. Isis called to me; she appeared in dreamtime. Since my passion and knowing of how dreams are a tool for us to see that which cannot be seen in waking life, I than realized she was speaking to me. She was calling me to my passion of listening, seeing, and hearing the soul (psyche) speak to me with all its glorious symbols. If she represents the archetype of dream healing as Asclepius does, than I must listen to their calling. My desire is to guide others in the realization that dreams are another instrument for healing and self-discovery. This dream lay in waiting for me to be united with Isis once again.

Upon our arrival and first meeting together with Dr. Tick, we were each asked to take the name of a Greek God or Goddess for the pilgrimage. This would be part of the embodiment of acting out the dream. I felt excited about the suggestion and couldn't wait for my turn to choose. Of course, when it got to me, the Goddesses I would have chosen were taken. I keep hearing Isis ringing in my ear and heart. I chose Isis, but with some hesitation.

I said, "I feel Isis is choosing me, but she is an Egyptian Goddess."

Dr. Tick then said that it was right for me to choose her and it would be revealed later why she was the right one to choose. He understood she was calling me into the mystery. I would find her on this journey where dreams become the medicine. This is how mystery is revealed, *yet still remains the mystery!* This was an invitation to enter a journey that is still continuing today. Life is a mystery, and isn't it amazing and wonderful that we can wake-up and participate.

When they show up in our dreams, what are they saying? What do they want? Each of us has our own answer to the dream and that is part of the mystery that is revealed. Asclepius and Isis, were they calling me to heal? Where they calling me to remember? Are they calling you? We just need to show up and remember who we are and where we stand in relationship to our healing.

Exercise For The Inner Healer

Before you go to bed take a few minutes to reflect, and in the silence allow a question regarding your health or someone you care about to come forth. This will be the question you will write down in your dream journal. Make the question short and direct. For example: What do I need to do to heal my wrist? You know what my answer was! Ask to remember your dream!

Upon waking write down your dream.

If nothing comes but feelings, then write that down: smells, feelings, and thoughts you might receive upon immediately waking. Those thoughts may be coming from a dream you cannot remember, so write them down. This is just the beginning. Practice, Practice, Practice!

Notes

Chapter Nine:
It's All In Our Perception

"Every noble thought in your mind brings you closer to God.
Those thoughts are like a river leading to the ocean of Spirit."

—*Paramahansa Yogananda*

Our perception of our reality will ultimately bring happiness or suffering. We always have the choice of how we perceive a situation. Now you may say, of course, when given such a choice, that you would always chose to be happy. You see, there are times when we create the situation where we become the victim, and there are other times when we are the victim of circumstances. Victim and co-creator come in many forms and situations in our lifetime. I have come to understand more clearly what that has meant to me in my life. I have had the opportunity to re-make my life over again and again by taking another look to see if I can perceive it with new eyes. Perhaps I am right in the middle of doing that at this very moment. Why not be open for the gift of that choice?

Remember what the indigenous people have taught, "If you can dream it, you can be it." I love to dream and move through the river of life with dreaming as my rudder. I know if I go with the flow and observe with open eyes what I face on my path, I have a better opportunity to bring happiness and peace into my life. The only thing I can't see is what's around the bend. This is a place on the river where I choose my thoughts wisely and bring the feelings of courage, faith and trust to move me with freedom toward the next bend. That is what builds character and strength. I know this as I have experienced it over and over. It is always okay, for it is all in *"The perception!"* How can we change the perception? We can learn to open ourselves to all directions, to having peripheral vision. We can leave out the *hindsight* — unless we look at it with *insight* — to greater understanding and clarity in our behavior.

I recall choices in my marriage that I believed had *only* one choice; I became a victim of circumstances. I felt trapped, forced into a choice that had been predetermined by my partner and yet, as I reflected upon it many years later, I realized I could have made another choice and had faith that my choice would benefit me in a greater way. That choice was not made; instead I made a choice out of *fear!* Was that the wrong choice? Perhaps not, but it *was* a choice, and it did change my life, at that time.

When we have the opportunity to reflect on choices made, we can usually see how we can let go of "the victim" and move forward with new understanding. We can grow from the struggle and heartache experienced. Those experiences have made me a woman of greater understanding and compassion for others. First, I had to take responsibility. I could carry the "wrong" choices around in a knapsack over my shoulder and be burdened for the rest of my life, but look at the pain and exhaustion that would be placed on my shoulders and radiate out to others around me! So, once again I share about "unpacking." We need to keep unpacking or that knapsack will become a trunk load of unnecessary burdens dragging us down.

I would like to share a dream that I had about fifteen years ago. It was an afternoon in the hot summer months while living in Florida. Of course, most of the months were hot summer months to me. I usually do not like to settle into a nap in the afternoon because I am always too busy, and also because they tend to leave me feeling uncomfortable and uneasy long after I awake. What generally can happen is a very unnerving dream that leaves me with deep emotion in the cellular body. What I recognize now is that they are usually "lucid dreams." Lucid dreams are those dreams where you are consciously dreaming; you are aware that you are dreaming, or you totally believe you are awake!

This one very hot summer afternoon I fell asleep and had the following dream:

I was observing the dining room in the home where I was living with my husband in Florida. (When I say observing, I mean I was actually viewing this scene from above. So, I was also viewing myself at the side of the table.) The table was set for a dinner party. I was off to one side of the table looking at the table and he was standing at the end of the table smiling, very pleased with what I had accomplished. Then the voice in the dream spoke to me, "If you do not change things, this is what will happen!" End of dream.

I awoke with an alarmed feeling of discomfort. I did not like the feeling of grief, sadness, and uneasiness I experienced. Knowing that my husband and I enjoyed entertaining I could not understand this dream. It almost had the emotion of a nightmare.

"If I did not change things, …" What did *that* mean? "…This is what will happen." *What will happen? More dinner parties?* More dinner parties would not change anything. Confused and baffled by this dream, I let it go. You see, looking at my husband and myself standing around the table smiling was not a big concern at that time. I did not look any deeper than what met the eye. I ignored the voice telling me to take a deeper look. *Never ignore the voice!* I have learned that one. I have also learned to recognize that voice. We could say it is our inner guide, our higher self, The Master. It is a knowing that I have come to recognize in dreamtime and waking. Later I came to realize that this had been a prophetic dream, yet there was no way I could see that at the time. There came a time, many years after the dream, when I met my ex-husband and his girlfriend. It was a very congenial meeting, but I had never seen a photograph of her prior, nor had anyone ever told me anything about her appearance. As I stood face to face with her, it was as if I were looking in a mirror! On this occasion of our meeting and spending several days together, we were asked over and over if we were sisters. Then, one day, someone asked if we were twins. WOW, what a "waking dream" this turned out to be. Dreams do come true. You know the expression: We all have a twin somewhere! I just never expected my ex-husband to find mine!

A few months later I recalled that dream and came to understand the vision and the voice in the dream. It did not make sense why I would want to change the situation in the joy of our entertaining, especially when he was so delighted with me. I never entertained the idea that there would be someone else in his life and that she would look like me — twins, sisters…. Perhaps if I had not been so stuck on thinking that the woman in the dream was me, I would have looked closer and noticed some difference or some sign that I was not that woman with my husband. Well, who knows where the dream can take us. Looking back, I had a choice. If *things* did not change, *the person in the dream would!*

If I had been honest with myself I would have looked at the relationship between my spouse and myself with deeper questioning. I would have questioned whether there was any truth to the appearance of the joy, peace and deep respect we held for each other in this dream. I would have said, *Barbara, I think you need a new perspective on this one. What image had each of us created that was not who we really were?* I needed to ask, *Are we truly seeing each other or are we only seeing the image we have created of each other?* I realize now that we may live with someone for twenty or thirty years and never recognize that we are only viewing the image we have created of them — our projection of them. First, we must know *ourselves!* When we do our own work, only then can we begin to open our hearts to understanding others. There are many times we seem to avoid looking honestly, therefore thinking things will change without understanding and questioning what both people want out of a relationship and life. Where I stand today, I often challenge myself with more honesty and questioning.

I have moved on from this dream, but it was a dream that has great meaning today. I shall always remember to question myself and look closely into the dream and listen to the voices that speak. We could refer to this as a prophetic dream or perhaps ... *dreaming ahead.* Either way, we can be given a little preview of what's to come. Movies always have them ... why not dreams?

If I had someone in my life at that time that worked closely with me with dreamtime, perhaps I could have understood or at least had the choice to see another perspective. I do now, and I ask you to dream and open your heart and mind to greater vision; dream so you can look at all of your choices. It is often wise to try on a new pair of glasses; they will perhaps give you a new perspective on where you stand.

LIFE IS BUT A DREAM AND YOU CAN CHANGE IT!

Exercise:

Remember a time or situation where you made a choice out of fear. Now you have an opportunity to create a new story. There are endless possibilities for this new story. How would this story begin, now that there is no fear? What great decision would you make, or adventure would you try, since there is no fear attached to the outcome?

Try dreaming ahead to a place where you have completed a task and the result is what you had hoped for, or even different but better. You may even try your hand at being an artist: painting, writing a book of poetry, pursuing photography, or a cooking a gourmet dish in your new kitchen. Dream Big!

Notes

Chapter Ten:
Guidelines for Navigating the River of Dreams

"I have dreamt in my life dreams that have stayed with me ever after, and
changed my ideas, they've gone through and through me, like wine through
water, and altered the color of my mind."

—Emily Bronte

There are many books on dream symbolism that can assist the new dreamer on the path. This is not that kind of book. This book has been written to share my story of how dreams have awakened me — and to show you how your dreams are speaking to you, as well. Paying attention to dreams has been a way for me to see more insightfully and has served me as a great tool for healing along the way. Dreaming has guided me into areas of exploration and self-discovery, clarity and understanding. Dreams have shown me how to navigate through the turbulent waters of life and have allowed me to find a calm and tranquil place to live, regardless of what is going on around me. I have come to a place in my life where I consciously seek my dreams rather than just waiting for spontaneous dreams to occur.

You may call it Conscious Dreaming. This process has transformed my perspective such that life is now a great, magical adventure, and I can't wait to see what the next chapter — the next dream — brings! This is my wish for you as well, and the following guidelines will serve to help you navigate the river of dreams that flows through your life.

1. You will need to make the waters peaceful — *meditate.*

I always meditate before going on my nighttime voyage. I find that I collect the struggles, experiences, challenges and the joys of the day; and then I release and let go. When the thoughts return, I continue to release and settle into a peaceful state. I may even ask for guidance or a message to be given to me while my ego consciousness is at rest. I often ask for messages for my highest good; may they be revealed and understood. I offer gratitude for the gifts and teachings I experienced that day. Whatever way you wish to complete your day will be your creative way. Take a few minutes to be silent; it's a great few minutes.

2. You will need a boat — *your journal will carry you upon these waters.*

Your journal will be the container for your nighttime voyage. I suggest you choose one that will fit next to your bed comfortably and be easy to carry with you when you travel away from home. I have found that some of my most informative dreams can come when I am traveling, when I am in unknown territory. It can open portals to new visions in dreamtime. The landscape in the physical world has changed and it creates an environment to welcome in new landscape for dreaming. My journal has become my personal calendar, in the sense that it holds the information of my activities while I sleep. There is a lot on the agenda!

3. You will need oars — *Your pen or pens will be your oars. They will draw your map.*

Choose the number and color of oars you wish to use to take you down the river. Sometimes I like to change the color of my pens, especially if I am headed in a direction of change; it draws my attention to different topics as I look back at myself ... in print. Color is also fun!

Now there will be times we may feel we are going upstream against the current, or we are getting off course; try not to be in fear, we can always get back on course. Keep letting go and going with the flow until the shift comes; you will then be going in the needed direction again. Sometimes going against the current is necessary for lessons in navigation technique. We are always learning new skills on this journey.

4. You will need information about this river — *Ask!*

You must ask the question if you want the answer! Every night before you go to bed, write down the question you want the answer to so that when you get an answer you are very clear on exactly what the question was. I am sure you want to know where you are headed. Perhaps you need to know about some illness that may have shown up while you were taking this journey in life. You see, this river is also a metaphor for life itself. We travel and we come to forks in the river that change direction into another tributary and then you are following another flow of the river. It's all connected, just as we are all connected. Sometimes we ask for directions and it takes some time for the answer to be shown to us. Try again. There are times I ask the same question over and over for three or four days. Then, when I am not even asking, it is revealed to me without asking again.

5. In order to arrive at your destination — *remember to write everything down.*

In order to remember, we must write it all down. Do not wait until the next morning. You will never remember. I remember hearing a very profound message, one time, being given to me in a dream and I thought, "I could never forget this!" Guess what? I did. I don't even know what I missed, except it was important! If you don't write it down right away, you will lose it. Train yourself to take the pen and paper in hand, quickly jot it down and then go right back to sleep. *You can write anywhere!* Don't even get up and go to the bathroom without the journal! Otherwise, the footsteps to and from the bathroom will have wiped your memory away. I never take the chance. I *am serious when I am navigating the river!* You can take it easy and choose how you like to navigate yours. I like to work with all the information that has been given to me, but each dreamer may choose their own course.

6. Remember, there are "signposts" along the way — *Look for them; they will guide you.*

Signs are literally everywhere! Sometimes they are subtle; sometimes they are bold, bright and hard to miss. Look for them as they will take you into uncharted waters where you may have never gone before. There you will find new choices and, when running into the rapids, do not fear as you will have learned many lessons when you arrive at the waters edge.

7. Remember to listen to that voice! — there may be a *warning* or some *guidance*.

As you practice this process of watching for the signposts and messages, the inner voice of wisdom will become recognizable. It will be known to you as clearly as if your best friend has called you on the phone — you simply know the voice without a doubt. Honoring the voice may be as simple as taking the time to write down what you heard so that, in time, you can receive validation that it actually was the voice of wisdom. You will only believe it if you prove it to yourself by writing it down and watching the mystery unfold as the message becomes validated.

8. You will need patience — *Don't ever give up!*

Patience is a *must* as there are many twists and turns on this river, and some areas, or lessons, may take a while to navigate. There is a great reward for patience and not giving up, and that is realization. When we have persisted and the day comes when we see the light shinning in the darkness upon what we could not understand, illuminating our understanding, Wow! It's worth it all!

9. You will need *TRUST* — *for you will not always know what is around the bend.*

This is a difficult one, I must admit, but there is no way to go with the flow without it. We will not always know what is around the bend, but trust, for me, represents a word of action. I am trusting and in that trust there is an inner knowing — a feeling of, "it is ok." I may have some sense about what is coming but I just can't quite see what is around the bend. However, I know it's where I need to go. Sometimes it feels we will never get around it, but we do. We've all heard the expression, "There is no way to the other side, but through," and it is equally applicable here. We need to keep going. There are times that we need a safe harbor in which to rest. Well, take time out if you need to. I have often said, "Hey, I need a break! No more dreams for the rest of the week!" You see, I can dream every night, twelve months a year. I need to know when to say, "Stop!" That also goes for giving ourselves some free time and remembering to always love ourselves "just the way we are." We know we still need work, but that is what we are here for on the journey.

10. You will need *FAITH* — *faith will help you to hold on so that you may realize your goal.*

You must have faith in order to see your work manifest into the physical reality. I have worked with it as a tool in my life. Sometimes that faith seems blind, but we learn how to recognize when faith comes from a deep heartfelt realization. For me, faith comes from the heart! Faith is an intuitive experience. If we are working to understand our minds and hearts, then we will learn the difference in that deep faith and trust. We may fall down a few times or more, but that is all in the learning process. Faith and trust can go hand and hand; some say that they are one and the same. I use them in slightly different ways. When all else fails and I have hit rock bottom or my world comes crashing down around me, I remember that innate quality of the soul: faith. You can nurture this quality by remembering it exists and that it is a tool within you. We become conscious and deeply aware the more we practice these tools for our transformation into extraordinary realities.

This is my waking dream for you:

May these tools guide you in The River of Dreams.   May they enrich your days ahead and bring your child-like curious nature into play, figuratively and literally. May fear begin to melt away into courage, strength, trust and faith. May you find forgiveness within this river for yourself and others in order to flow in peace and harmony with your true nature. May you find a place to *surrender* it all when you do not understand. You will not be "giving up;" *surrender* is a powerful *action*. May your dreams truly alter the color of your mind with awakened joy, beauty, peace and love.

Chapter Eleven:
Living In "Dreamland"

"Sometimes Dreams are Wiser than Waking"

—Black Elk, Ogala Sioux

Life continues to be full of "surprises," and unfolds in perfect timing. It keeps us on our toes, reminding us to live our truth.

As I came to this final chapter of my book, I was challenged with the last important words to leave with, you, my readers. I wanted a "last chapter," then realized the story is never over. I did find myself wondering, with that certain "knowing" I speak about, if something was missing; I couldn't figure out what it was. I was working long hours with a passion to present a manuscript that had a story told with heart, but felt it was incomplete. I began to search my heart, asking myself what was it that I was trying to say to my readers. I questioned whether the message was complete, in as much as I knew to be my expression of truth. I knew that I had come to the classic "writer's block," and finally surrendered it all.

I wrote to Eve, my editor, and said, "I will be in touch tomorrow and let you know what I feel. I hope that I am not "Living in Dreamland" about all of this! I truly want this to be a book that will touch people and open them up to a new vision for themselves. I want them to realize that they can *move mountains and see the river that connects to the source that moves within us.* I want to assist in bringing their dreams into the light so that they can bring forth the information that is hidden behind their busy daytime minds. I wish to share this gift we all have, for experiencing greater understanding, insight and clarity. I have moved those mountains and the river now flows with insight!" I sent the e-mail off and then realized that while I had made the "Living in Dreamland" comment sarcastically, as if it was a negative, what I was sharing in this book was my gift of dreaming as a great tool for insight into the land of dreams. This is a place where we can discover who and what lives inside of us. Not only was I truly "Living in Dreamland," but that is exactly what I was teaching others to do as well! In that moment, I decided to practice what I was teaching in order to resolve this question. I closed the manuscript and took my dream journal in hand and wrote, "What needs to be shared in this last chapter?" I laid the pen and journal down and traveled off to dreamland.

Upon waking at 7:30 am on Saturday, October 28th , I took pen in hand and this is what I wrote — my dream:

The voice had spoken, "Summary of where you came from and where you are!" Then the stage was set and the actors appeared as follows: I was arriving at a hotel with three other people. The hotel was very large and it was spread out over a lot of land. The hotel seemed to be part outdoors and part indoors. We were being seated at a table for four. It was very lovely and we were in a small outside area, but I was very interested in seeing the rest of the land this hotel sat upon, as well as the hotel itself. There was so much to explore. The people I was with were content staying where they were and didn't want to go with me, so I left my cup of coffee and walked away. I thought I would be back. It was a long walk to the other side, and along the way I visited all the land that this hotel covered. It was full of interesting things, but some were very strange. I realized that some of the things I saw were real and some were not. I saw two cows, one on each side of the land I was walking across. "Very interesting," I thought and continued to walk. I got to the other side and was seated, however, there were people who wanted to join me and we began to enjoy the food and many wonderful things that were offered over on this side. There was so much more. I began to realize this was the place where I wanted to stay. It was wonderful and each new thing that I discovered was more interesting and nourishing. The place I had taken to occupy on this side was "inside" the hotel. The inside was warm and beautiful and full of wonder. I thought, "WOW, the inside and the outside were beautiful and it's all part of this Grand Hotel!"

I thought about the people I had come with, that did not want to join me on this other side of the hotel, and I wanted to invite them over to join me. I realized that I could not be seated at two tables at the same time on opposite sides of the hotel. I had to choose one. The one I had found on the inside was the one with all the wonder and the expanded view. I got up from the table and started to travel back across the land to meet them and share this wonder. As I walked past the cows, they seemed to be little pieces of hay coming from their mouths and it was as if they were watering the earth. I could not get around them. I knew I would get wet from the watering, but I had to just go through in order to get to the other side. I was not too happy about that as I felt that I would get dirty and not be presentable when I got back to the other three that were waiting. I just walked through it all, however, got wet and it was all ok. I began to realize there was too much space between the two sides. I could not keep going back and forth between the two. When I got back I realized I could not take my

cup of coffee with me. I was being nourished with new food and something
new was quenching my thirst! I then woke up!

I realized that this dream supplied the answer to my question! This
dream offered the last chapter in this book! What better way could I
share how I have used my dreams to help me see what I could not see
in the daytime than to show how I receive the messages by "*Asking*"!

So, here is how I understood the dream and what it revealed to
me: I arrived at the hotel with three other people. They were "most
likely" my husband, son and daughter. You see, it was a table for four
and that made up our family, so this is what my dream was showing
me. I recognized how small the area was where we were seated and also
recognized the hotel was large with lots of land incorporated into it. I
wanted to expand and explore all that was available and I saw glimpses
of that view. This place incorporated both "inside" and "outside." As
I have mentioned in earlier chapters, I wanted to live from the "inside
out." To live from the inside out, I would need to visit all that existed
within the hotel and on all the land that surrounded and incorporated
the hotel. This hotel represented a place for tremendous growth. It had
many levels to it and had several dinning rooms. I did not want to
stay in the dinning area that was limiting my view. This Grand Hotel
represented the universe as well as representing me. I did not know
what was inside the place I wanted to explore. I did not know how far
it was to get to see what was there, but I didn't want to be limited. I got
up and left the three people behind and the unfinished cup of coffee,
but felt I would return after I saw the *whole place.* You could say, I was
searching for wholeness and that had to come from looking inside.

I started the journey across the land and realized it was a long
walk. Just as in this dream, the journey takes time and we often do
not recognize the distance that must be traveled to view the inside

of such a Grand Hotel. The land I walked was very diverse and there were two cows, one on each side of the land I traveled. Cows, have a specific meaning to me, as I see them as most of us do, as nurturing and feeding us. For myself they also mean "The Sacred." In fact I have a white cowhide in my living room and I call it my Sacred Cow. That comes from the Indian influence in my life, both Native American and East Indian. This is what I meant in Chapter Six, when I spoke about creating our own symbolic dictionaries along the way. Always ask what the symbols in your dreams mean to you.

When I arrived at the hotel I was guided and shown a place I could be seated with other people who were also in search of this Grand Hotel, and they were enjoying the food that was being served. I see this part as a place where I have been guided to join people of "like mind" and we were being fed from the same source! It was abundant and there was more than enough for all of us. Isn't that how Spirit feeds us?! There is always enough and no one is left unnourished, however, we need to enter the room where we can be fed. We must each look for the place that feeds our body and soul, and that may be slightly different for each of us. As I sat and was being fed and offered an invitation to see more, I realized I had left the other three on the other side. I wanted to share with them what I had *realized* was available for all of us in this place of beauty, although it is a long journey to get to that *realization!* I then thought to myself, "You must go back and share what you have found." I started back across the land to invite them to join me. I saw the two cows — Nurturing and Sacred! They were watering the land from their mouths and the water was hay. *Wow*, here is another realization that I knew was truth in understanding this symbol. What we speak from our mouths waters the seeds that will sprout and grow. Here I also realized that what we eat (what we are fed) is what will in return water the seeds. So, hay in — hay out! I knew what I fed myself would be what

I could nurture myself on and in return nurture the seeds in others. What was truth here? What I may have watered in the past may not have been all the good seeds. Perhaps there were negative seeds watered and that was something to look at, as I was doing in this dream. In this part of the dream I did not want to get wet or dirty — what would they think? Well, sometimes we just need to jump in and know that we are not always going to be clean in the action we take. But we do need to go forward and know that the only way is through, even if we must get wet! We can't always worry about what others will think of how we appear. We just need to come from a place of honesty and truth from our hearts. That is the *Sacred Place.*

Then, I arrived back at the table I had left. I asked if they would like to join me across the land to see the "whole hotel." I heard no reply in the dream, but I was told by an inner voice that I could not take my coffee with me to the other side. I had to leave it behind. Well, another personal dream symbol out of my dictionary! Coffee is something I enjoy, and at times I have enjoyed it too much. I guess I became addicted to the taste. I would say that was a metaphor for the things I enjoyed and did not want to leave behind. Such as the life style and people I had become accustomed to and wanted to take with me. I was not allowed that cup of coffee to travel with me. I was given a new taste of life and a new cup to drink from. I could say in a soul sense, my cup now is often full, but we also know that it can be empty from the grief and pain of the world today. I try to remember to open up and allow the cup to be replenished. We can help fill the cup of one another. When I arrived back at the hotel, I realized I was being fed with new food, and something new was quenching my thirst! I woke up!

I have come to realize the truth of Roshi Joan's words, *"If you are looking for enlightenment, you have missed it."* I have traveled a long distance over this earth and in my heart. I will tell you this, I am no longer "looking for enlightenment," as I am trying to *live* what I had been *looking for*. My dreams, as I have mentioned, are one of my most valuable tools for helping me to do this. They are the way I receive my messages so I can look deeper and move forward. We all are looking for truth in our lives and there is a search and longing to find that which nurtures us and feeds us.

I have looked at where I was thirty years ago, or even last year, and I realize I have grown beyond the limitations that held me captive in the cage I created. We cannot go back, but we can *reflect* upon those things in life that have given us the opportunity for growth. I do not stay in guilt or blame, as that will bring suffering into my life and block my journey forward. I realize that I must greet everyday as a new opportunity on this river of life, and embrace the sorrow and joy as one. Each day is a spiritual day! This realization is truly in waking and saying, "Thank you for this day." I will do the best I can with what I am given.

So, where am I now? "Living in Dreamland" has caused life to become more peaceful. I know that I am still guided with the faith that each day gives me the opportunity to share my story and live a life of "mindfulness." I have learned to have fun alone when no one can join me. I have learned to enjoy the quiet times alone. I have learned to enjoy a cup of tea (rather than just coffee) as the sun rises and sets on each day. Most of all I have learned to *love my self* just the way I am. Everyday is a good day since each day I am learning more about who I am. What is inside of us needs to be brought out into the fresh air of life so we can take a deep breath and continue our journey. We must see it fresh with new eyes and an open *heart*. Living in the flow of the river of dreams has added the elements of joy and excitement to my life. There is no denying that there is a greater mystery being revealed nightly. When I listen and pay attention, I discover that this mysterious river of dreams is teaching and guiding me, helping me to make sense of my waking state. I revel in the depth of self-discovery that unfolds as I "unpack" the messages that I have been given. I am continuously amazed by the recognition that our lives are not random circumstance. The connections are vast and almost unfathomable, and events are often foreseen in dreams years before they happen in the waking world..

I am joyfully still learning and dreaming in this river. I continue to ask for understanding and wisdom, to *"Live From The Inside Out!"* I believe that each one of us has a thread to weave into the creation we call *the universe.* This is the way we will co-create with God, our world … a peaceful self .. . a peaceful world, one dream at a time. We can wake up and dream with open eyes and listening hearts. This is my truth … This is *my Dream.*

WHAT IS YOUR DREAM?

DREAM JOURNEY

I awake to my dream as I slumber into the
Rivers of my journey

I sleep and go deep into my world where
I keep the shadow hidden in corners
In boxes and the closets of
My life

I peek through the opening of my dreams
There I see the stars and galaxies that guide
The pages of my evening journal of
Knowledge and wisdom

I walk the pages of life's experiences
I realize the climb up the mountain and the
Swimming upstream leads to
Understanding and wisdom

I view the labyrinth that I must walk in reverse
To be back at the beginning
Where I always existed
I now realize when the river meets the ocean
I am awake

Printed in the United States
90711LV00004B/40-138/A